Leadi
— a step by step

and
building your leadership skills

ISBN 978-1481807678 Second Edition

Copyright 2012 by Dave Douglas and Douglas Enterprises
Incorporated

6825 Harrop Procter Rd, Nelson, B.C. Canada V1L 6R2

www.leadingtheway-book.com

Praise for *Leading the Way*

Leadership is a skill that is developed and honed from many years of experience and honest craftsmanship. There can be no finer example than the author of this book of the character and qualifications necessary to provide guidance to others on how to build a framework for leadership success. All who read this book and follow the suggestions and ideas will be better for having done so and will set themselves on a path to excellence and self fulfilment.

*—Gary Gumley, president of
Interactive Learning Corporation*

I really, really enjoyed reading this. In fact, it took me a while to go through it as I kept stopping to do all your activities—I loved them! I found this really helpful personally, as I'm sure would your target group. It is a really good read and it has helped me think through who I am and what I want—no doubt it will help others too!

*—Dr. Jennifer Chapman
Washington DC*

This is certainly a book I would enjoy reading as a college student or a young adult just entering the career field. It has loads of insight and practical steps towards improving leadership skills…It has accurately captured the [need for] stepping up to the plate and guiding others towards greater goals.

—Christy Poirier

This [book] brings up important questions that this group may not necessarily have contemplated seriously at this point in their lives … excellent thought-provoking and motivating questions.

—Stacey Semenoff , 4th year university student

There are so many leadership opportunities around and a book like this is great for giving people the tools they need to take on leadership roles…this book is filled with useful information, good examples and plenty of encouragement.

—Allison, high school student

It made me stop and think about how I could be a better person.

—Tyler, high school student

…it's very inspiring—explains many things about leadership that I didn't know.

—Cindy, high school student

…it will help people who want to become leaders be more effective and successful.

—Samantha, high school student

This book opening my eyes to what leadership is all about. I can hardly wait to get a copy of the finished book!

—John, university student

I really enjoyed reading this [book]. It has encouraged me to become a more effective leader.

—Amanda, high school student

INTRODUCTION

Leading the Way is a book about leadership and developing your leadership skills. It has been written in response to the many requests I have received, as well as to record information regarding aspects of leadership that I have presented, been part of presenting, or have learned
over many years in senior leadership roles.

While it is impossible, in a small book like this, to cover the complete realm of leadership in exhaustive detail, I have tried to capture the essence of the subject and provide you with glimpses from my perspective of the more important aspects. As you will discover, each of the many topics discussed in the book could be an entire book on its own.

I have included a number of questions, activities and exercises in the book, identified as Action Steps, to challenge and assist you in exploring how you fit within the different aspects of leadership. They will help you focus on who you are and where you are in your life as a leader.

Leading the Way is made up of five sections:

Section 1—What is Leadership?
In this section you will learn about: what leadership is; examples of influential leaders; defining leadership; leading versus managing; leadership opportunities; leadership styles; leadership power bases; characteristics of effective leaders, and leadership ethics.

Section 2—Defining Your Leadership Style
In this section you will explore: who you are; what influences who you become; developing beliefs and values; methods to reflect on these things, and journaling.

Section 3—Developing Your Leadership Skills
In this section you will learn: how you can build on your leadership skills and focus on four key skills: communication,

critical thinking, decision making and working with people/groups. You will also learn about the value of mentors, how to find them and things to consider when selecting them.

Section 4—Where Are You Going?

In this section you will learn about the importance of goal setting and overcoming negatives and obstacles. You will also be introduced to the process I teach and use myself for setting goals.

Section 5—How Do You Get There?

In this section you will learn how to establish strategies to accomplish your goals. You will also learn about action planning, visualization techniques and developing your personal mission statement.

The basic skills you learn from this book should be all you need to begin your journey as a leader. As a young person in today's society, you will face numerous opportunities to utilize your leadership skills and experience the challenges and successes that come from that. I trust that as you work your way through this book, the action steps and questions, you will discover that if you want to be a truly effective leader, it will be a lifelong study.

Turn to page 1 and begin your journey! Make sure you have paper and a pen or pencil so you can respond to the action steps.

TABLE OF CONTENTS

SECTION 1
WHAT IS LEADERSHIP?

"IT IS ONE OF THE MOST BEAUTIFUL
COMPENSATIONS IN LIFE . . . . .
WE CAN NEVER HELP ANOTHER, WITHOUT HELPING
OURSELVES"
— Ralph Waldo Emerson

LEADERSHIP IS ABOUT making a difference. Whether you are a student, athlete, employee, volunteer or a member of a group or organization, you **can** make a difference. It could be a difference in your life as you journey to where you are going and determining how you will get there. It could be a difference in the lives of your family, friends, teammates and/or workmates as you interact with them, encouraging and challenging them to attain their goals.

Leadership is also about being forward-looking or visionary. For yourself that means looking at where you want to go or how you want to be and then going for it. If you are leading a team or group it is determining where you would like the group to go, communicating that to the group, then inspiring them to work towards that goal.

There is no perfect formula for becoming an effective leader, and there is no perfect way to be one. As you study famous leaders you have read about or those who have impacted your life directly, you will learn that leaders come in all ages, sizes, ethnic backgrounds, and personalities. They can be loud or quiet, encouraging or demanding. They are not always positive role models either -- look at Adolf Hitler and Osama Bin Laden .

Here are two leaders that have influenced many of us and the characteristics they have that I believe are most important:

Mother Teresa — compassion, empathy, caring & competent.

Mother Teresa's work has been recognised and acclaimed throughout the world. She has received numerous awards and distinctions, including the Pope John XXIII Peace Prize, the Nehru Prize for her promotion of international peace and understanding and the Nobel Peace Prize. On October 7, 1950, Mother Teresa started her own order, Missionaries of Charity, whose primary task was to love and care for those persons nobody else is prepared to look after. In 1965 the Society became an International Religious Family by a decree of Pope Paul VI; it now operates throughout the world, aided and supported by "Co-Workers," volunteers who serve those in need in their neighborhoods and towns. Mother Teresa died on September 5, 1997.at the age of 87.

Mother Teresa

"DO NOT WAIT FOR LEADERS; DO IT ALONE, PERSON BY PERSON."

— Mother Teresa

Oprah Winfrey — encouraging, supportive, caring & giving

Oprah Winfrey is an American media personality, actress, television producer, literary critic and magazine publisher. She is best known for her self-titled, multi-award winning talk show, which became the highest-rated program of its kind in history. She overcame adversity, including being abused as a child, to be ranked the richest African American of the 20th century, the first African American to be one of America's top philanthropists, and was once the world's only black billionaire. According to many, she is the most influential woman in the world.

Oprah Winfrey

"THE WHOLE PURPOSE OF BEING ALIVE IS TO EVOLVE INTO THE COMPLETE PERSON"
— Oprah Winfrey

Here are some young (Generation Y) leaders that through their leadership have made a difference in the lives of many others:

Ashley Dennehy – visionary, difference maker

Ashley Dennehy, a young woman from the Samson Cree Nation in Hobbema, Alberta is making a difference in her life, and the lives of many others. At the age of 23 Ashley stepped out of her comfort zone and applied for an internship to train to work with *Women for Change* in *Zambia.* She undertook intensive training for 4 weeks in Victoria, B.C. and along with 9 other Interns travelled to Africa in February, 2012.

Training for her internship was provided by the Victoria International Development Association (VIDEA) with funding provided by the Government of Canada through CIDA (Canadian International Development Association).

During her internship Ashley developed papers to inform and sensitize donors, stakeholders and the general public about a number of issues in Africa, including;
- climate change and its effect on marginalized groups.
- gender based violence and its cyclic role in poverty.

She also distributed information about human rights along with resource materials provided by *Woman for Change* into the operational areas she visited.

Here is how Ashley describes her 4 months in Africa:
"When I was in Africa, it was a lonely journey - but I believe it was all for a greater good, not only for the people I met and worked with there, but for the people of my community as well.

It is like the metaphor of the rock dropped into a pond with its rippling effect. The experience, I describe as the rock, providing me with the tools and skills to learn, and jumping into the experience as the rock dropping into the pond. The rippling effect is all the doors that have opened to me both in Africa and back home in my own community. This experience changed my life, I felt that the Creator wouldn't give me anything I couldn't handle, said Ashley. I was challenged every day, but the challenges led to life lessons I needed to learn.

The skills I learned in Zambia working with Women for Change, empowering women there, and studying the issues of sustainability, I am bringing back to my community to make it a more sustainable First Nation."

Ashley playing Stella Ella Ola (in the Losi Language) with children in Senanga

Ashley is continuing to make a difference since returning from Africa:

- starting her own non-profit organization with a focus on empowering women and young girls in her community.
- partnering with an engineer and other non-profit groups - utilizing her own designs, they are developing sustainable housing – the first of its kind for First Nation peoples.
- participated in fundraising for youth programming for her community and the Edmonton Inner-city.
- recently completed a clothing drive for the Edmonton Inner-city
- seeking funding support to donate a water well for the Lundazi District in Zambia as well as solar panels for the school located there.

- working with Samson Schools to "twin" with a school in Zambia.

Ashley's advice to young people, especially First Nations youth, is to "leap at every opportunity, and trust in the Creator's plans for you." "Take chances and if you make mistakes, don't beat yourself up – the mistakes are only lessons learned." "When things are easy, that is the path you need to follow, if things are difficult and hard, perhaps that is not the path the creator intends for you."

"As an Indigenous person helping other Indigenous people (my brothers and sisters in Africa and in my community) it feels amazing to give a hand up, not a hand out."

"BE THE CHANGE YOU WISH TO SEE IN THE WORLD"
— Mahatma Ghandi

Ashley Dennehy

Isaiah Qualls — Difference Maker

Isaiah, from Moscow, Idaho, a recent high school grad, and currently attending the University of Idaho, is making a big difference in the world. Isaiah is the founder and a director of a non-profit project called *"The Water Fight"*. Since its establishment in December 2010, *"The Water Fight"* has completed 19 water wells in Africa. Focusing on an agricultural region of Kenya called Tulwet, they work with the Water Commissioner and Village Elders to strategically saturate the area with clean water. Their goal is to place 100 wells in this area.

They have implemented a *Well Cooperative System* that helps groups of neighbors (usually 10) to purchase their own well materials (approx $120 US). *"The Water Fight"* crew (who are from Kenya) train the people as they establish the first three wells, then the persons who have been trained, provide the labor for each other as they finish the other seven. The well users are also trained in how to use and maintain the wells, with all parts available from local hardware stores. This method is not only efficient but is empowering for the local African people. The total cost for completion of each well is approximately $1,000.00 and take approximately 2 – 4 days to complete. With one well serving up to 500 people it is making a significant difference for the people there.

Africa became part of Isaiah's life when two young men from Sodda Wolaita, a small village in southern Ethiopia, became part of his family in 2006. He travelled to Africa for the first time in December 2010 with his father and some friends from Seattle. They flew to Nairobi, Kenya, and then drove north towards Kisumu to a small village called Dago.

Here is how Isaiah describes this experience; "What began there in that little village in Africa has changed my life path forever. When I came home I couldn't wrap my head around what I had just experienced. I was devastated. I thought how could I go on living when the friends I met there are dying". Isaiah posted the following on Facebook a few days after the trip; "the truth is I can't say my eyes were opened. I already knew what level of suffering people there were experiencing; the pain, death and disease. The only difference now is those people are my friends, and I just can't turn my back like I used to".

Isaiah worked for a construction company that summer and for a few weeks was working on a roof tearing off shingles in 90 degree heat and being covered in tar dust- it was a growing experience, but he had time to think. He had one year left of high school and just wanted to know, "what is it that I am here for?" Isaiah says, "I think that is something we all want to know – it's fundamental to our existence." He began to ask God where do you want me to go/do. Sometime later and after much soul searching Isaiah decided that he could do something to help his friends in Africa from home and in December *"The Water Fight"* was born. Reaching out to students in America Isaiah has challenged them to support their brothers and sisters in Africa by generating funding to provide wells. Isaiah says, "Changing lives in Africa – changes our own lives".

To learn more about *"The Water Fight"* and to hear Isaiah speak about their program Google their web page at http://thewaterfight.org .

Isaiah says that 884 million people lack access to clean water – 1 in 8 people on the planet, and every 14 seconds, a child dies from the effects of dirty water. You can be a difference maker as well. I am sure that Isaiah would welcome your support.

Isaiah Qualls

Jeneece Edroff — fundraising phenom, prolific philanthropist, courageous

Jeneece, a 15 year old girl, was chosen to light the Olympic torch for the start of the 45,000km Olympic Torch Relay for the 2010 Winter Olympics. She was chosen for this honor because of the charity work she does in spite of a chronic illness

At the age of three, Jeneece Edroff was diagnosed with neurofibromatosis type 1 (NF1), a debilitating genetic disease. In her case, tumors grow from the nerve tissues in her spine, causing her vertebrae to become thin and unsupported. After several surgeries, doctors believed she would never walk again and told her parents it was unlikely she would live to be a teenager. True to her nature, she would later run into the surgeon's office to thank him for "helping me walk again."

At the age of seven while using her third back brace, Edroff realized just how much that Variety, a children's charity, was helping her family with the costs related to her illness. She began a penny drive at her school and later presented $164 to Variety during its Show of Hearts Telethon. The following year, with assistance from a local news anchor, she received sixteen tons of pennies, resulting in a contribution of $27,000 to Variety, later matched during the telethon to $54,000. Over the years, the Jeneece and Friends Coin Drive has raised over $1.5 million for Variety.

Since 2009, Edroff has been fundraising for her own dream: Jeneece Place, a home away from home for kids and families traveling to Victoria for medical care. Her story inspired TELUS, a Canadian telecommunications firm and AFP's 2010 Outstanding Corporation, to get involved. A partnership developed between Edroff, the Queen Alexandra Foundation for Children (QAF) and TELUS that resulted in TELUS selecting Jeneece Place to receive the $1 million proceeds from its 2010 World Skins Gold Tournament.

Since her dream of Jeneece Place began, Edroff has been working to help raise the $5.5 million needed to build it. Vancouver Island's Norgaard Foundation announced a $1 million gift, which was matched by Queen Alexandra Foundation. Jeneece Place opened in January, 2012, allowing up to 600 families per year to have a place to call home when they face a medical crisis.

Janeece has inspired Canadians to give more than $6.7 million in contributions to help children.

Jeneece was awarded the order of British Columbia in 2010, the youngest recipient ever to be so honored and in 2011 the Association of Fundraising Professionals presented her with the Changing Our World/Simms Award for Outstanding Youth in Philanthropy, Ages 5-17.

To learn more about Jeneece and her amazing projects check her web page at:
http://www.rwglobal.com/~jeneece/index.html

Jeneece – wearing her Order of B.C. Medal

Craig & Marc Kielburger — dedicated, focused, difference makers

Craig Kielburger is the founder & Chairperson of **Free The Children.** He established this charity in 1995 at the age of 12. It is the world's largest network of children helping children through education. Craig has received numerous awards including the Nelson Mandela Human Rights award, the World Economic Forum GLT award to mention 2, received two honorary doctorates degrees and been nominated three times for the Nobel Peace Prize.

Marc Kielburger is the Chief Executive Director of **Free The Children** and cofounder & Chief Executive Director of **Leaders Today,** one of the top youth leadership training organizations in the world. He has received an honorary doctorate of education for his work in leadership development.

Craig and Marc Kielburger coauthored the bestselling book "**ME TO WE**" which has been featured on **Oprah.** To learn more about the Kielburger's and Me to We - check their web page at: http://www.metowe.com/

Marc Kielburger and Craig Kielburger

ACTION STEP 1

Take a few moments to reflect on someone who has impressed you as an effective leader (whether you have read about them or know them personally), and see if you can identify specific qualities, characteristics or traits that have influenced you. Write them in your Action Guide. Include their names and positions.

Review this step as you learn to recognize the qualities of effective leadership.

Note: While I mention writing your responses in the Action Guide, it is not essential. You may record your answers to the Action Steps in a notebook, journal, your computer or however you wish. If you are interested in obtaining a copy of the Action Guide in a downloadable Word format, please visit our web page at www.leadingtheway-book.com.

When looking for leaders, don't forget about your own community – Scout and Guide Leaders, coaches, the mayor, or business leaders for example. Analyze what qualities and characteristics they have that make them successful and effective leaders.

The key to understanding how to be an effective leader is to first understand who you are so that you can formulate your own effective style. As you go through this book you will be looking at your strengths, weaknesses, values and beliefs. You will look at where are you going in life and how will you get there. Section 2 will provide you with tools and suggestions to assist you in that discovery.

You will determine your own unique style. Then you can learn the many skills that will assist you, such as critical thinking, decision making, adaptability and effective communication skills.

ACTION STEP 2

Here is a personal challenge for you. What qualities or characteristics do you feel you have that would enable you to become an effective leader? Don't be afraid to identify your qualities and see yourself in a positive leadership role.
Take a moment to write these qualities and characteristics in your Action Guide. We will refer to them later in this section.

LEADERSHIP DEFINED

There are as many definitions for leadership as there are leaders. Here are two for your consideration:

The book **The Leader in You**, by Dale Carnegie and Associates Inc., says:

"WHAT'S NEEDED IS LEADERSHIP, TO HELP PEOPLE
ACHIEVE WHAT THEY ARE CAPABLE OF,
TO ESTABLISH A VISION FOR THE FUTURE,
TO ENCOURAGE, TO COACH ANDTO MENTOR,
AND ESTABLISH AND MAINTAIN SUCCESSFUL
RELATIONSHIPS"

The following one is by Warren Bennis, Professor of Business Administration at USC, who is regarded as a pioneer in the contemporary field of Leadership Studies. He has written over two dozen books on leadership, change and creative groups.

"LEADERSHIP IS A FUNCTION OF KNOWING YOURSELF,
HAVING A VISION THAT IS WELL COMMUNICATED,
BUILDING TRUST AMONG COLLEAGUES AND
TAKING EFFECTIVE ACTION TO REALIZE
YOUR OWN LEADERSHIP POTENTIAL"

As you develop your leadership skills you will no doubt run across many other definitions. You may even develop one of your own that matches your own style. If you do, it should become part of your personal mission statement. A personal mission statement is rather like your own personal constitution: the basis by which you consider and evaluate what you wish to accomplish and contribute in your life. A detailed outline of what a personal mission statement is and how to develop your own is included at the end of Section 5 in this book.

LEADERS OR MANAGERS

Leaders and managers have two different roles. This comparison between a leader and manager is not meant to downplay the role of managers; they play a key role in keeping things in order and on track.

Mangers do provide leadership when required. However, as this is a book on leadership and what makes an effective leader, I have identified the difference from my perspective, so as to help clarify the leadership role.

Leaders need to ask themselves whether they are going to lead the staff that report to them or just manage them. Leading involves providing the vision and inspiration for the group – and knowing when to lead, follow or get out of the way. Leaders – when they have defined their vision and shared it with their people – stand back and let them get on with the work required. They make themselves available to assist and guide when obstacles are encountered.

On the other hand, managing is arranging to get the work done by directing those whom they lead. It is arranging for the necessary workers and resources required – then telling the workers what is to be done. Managers tend to keep involved after assigning the work to ensure it is being done in the manner directed.

This comparison is not meant to downplay the role of Managers, as they play a key role in keeping things in order and on track. They do provide leadership when required.

In his book, "On Becoming a Leader", Warren Bennis says, "I tend to think of the differences between leaders and managers as the difference between those who master the context (*the setting in which they work"*) and those who surrender to it." He goes on to define the differences. I have listed them below:

Leader	**Manager**
innovates	administers
is an original	is a copy
develops	maintains
focuses on people	focuses on systems & structure
inspires trust	relies on control
has a long-range perspective	has a short-range view
asks what and why	asks how and when
eye on the horizon	eye on the bottom line
originates	imitates
challenges the status quo	accepts the status quo
is his/her own person	classic good soldier
does the right thing	does things right

"MANAGEMENT IS EFFICIENCY IN CLIMBING THE LADDER OF SUCCESS; LEADERSHIP DETERMINES WHETHER THE LADDER IS LEANING AGAINST THE RIGHT WALL"

— Stephen R, Covey

LEADERSHIP OPPORTUNITIES

Leadership opportunities can be found everywhere. You can take a leadership role:

- in your own family by setting an example for your parents, siblings, roommates, children, etc.
- among a group of friends.
- at school with teams, student groups and other organizations.
- at work – by example when you first start a job (work ethic), and then by accepting more responsibilities as you move up the ladder.
- through various volunteer activities (in school and community)

You have probably been in teams or groups where one of your friends or teammates was constantly encouraging the rest of your group. They may have been the captain or president of your group or maybe just one of the team. Or you may know someone in your school, university, work, or community that has shown leadership in an activity or event, encouraging others and urging them to work hard. Has a parent, sibling or close relative challenged or encouraged you or others to do well?

STEALTH LEADERSHIP

Leadership is responding to a need within a group that has a defined goal or objective they are striving to attain. Stealth leadership is responding to a situation that needs attention at the time it is observed. It is where you take action not expecting (or wanting) recognition or remuneration. It is what you are willing to do on behalf of others — when no one is there to check up on you or force you to do it. This could be as simple as picking up trash on the street and putting it in a garbage can or recycling bin, helping an elderly person carry their groceries to the car, opening a door for someone or doing chores around the house without being asked. Keep alert for opportunities to provide such a service and don't expect recognition. You will not only set a good example you will learn to become grateful when you observe others doing similar things.

Adam Robertson, a good friend of mine and one of my mentors, never passed a child's lemonade stand without stopping to buy lemonade. He believed strongly in encouraging and mentoring children from an early age.

I RECOMMEND YOU TRY IT, NOT ONLY WILL YOU ENCOURAGE A CHILD – YOU WILL FEEL GOOD.

One thing I have done over the years is to plug the parking meter of someone whose time has expired so they don't receive a ticket. They don't know who did that for them and it brings a smile to my face knowing I have made a small difference.

Here are a few examples of people using different opportunities to demonstrate leadership:

When she was about 10, our daughter Laura provided valuable leadership within our family. At a family meeting to discuss goals and assign chores, she raised the issue of recycling – something we were not very diligent about at that time. We immediately embarked on a program and have been doing it consciously ever since.

An article in The Times Colonist, our local Newspaper featured a 6 year- old- girl named Hannah who wanted to raise money for charity. She set up a lemonade stand in front of her house, taking advantage of a plant sale next door and raised $267.00 – all of which she donated to the local food bank.

During a National Volunteer Week, Bilaal Rajan a grade 8 student in Markham Ontario shed his shoes and went barefoot to raise awareness of children in poverty who can't afford shoes. Bilaal has been helping to raise funds for various causes since he was 4 years old and has published a book titled ***Making Change: Tips from an Underage Overachiever***.

Fourteen-year-old Kristen, from Pennsylvania, records the thoughts and stories of some World War II and Korean War veterans. "I think it will give the youth of my community a better understanding of what happened during the war. Hopefully, it will also give us a greater respect to the men and woman lives so we can be who sacrificed their time, effort, support and sometimes free today."

Opportunities may be ongoing or arise on a one time basis at any time – you never know. Just be prepared to jump in and lead.

LEADERSHIP STYLES

Most people in leadership circles talk about three main leadership styles: Autocratic, Democratic and Laissez-faire.

- ***Autocratic*** – the leader makes all the decisions and demands appropriate responses from team member. Examples of where this type of Leadership is used include the military, a newspaper or other media corporation (in order to meet a publishing deadline), or in emergency situations that require an urgent response such a hospital Emergency Department .

- ***Democratic or Participative*** – while the leader retains final responsibility, team members are asked for their ideas and input, often voting to determine the best course of action to take. This generally encourages members to have more ownership of the decisions agreed upon. Because the group members have an equal say in the decisions being made they are generally more committed to the work. When used correctly this is the best style for most situations. An example of this style of leadership could be a school setting where the principal meets with department heads and staff to talk about implementing a new program, and seeks input from everyone. Then they vote as a group to decide whether or not the wish to implement the program. The principal retains the final responsibility for the decision based on the discussion and the vote that has taken place.

- *Laissez*-**faire**- literally means "let it be." This style is where the leader monitors the work and provides feedback when required, but encourages the members of the group to work independently and to make decisions on their own. This requires the leader to have implicit trust in the team members and a highly motivated group of individuals. This works best for groups where the individuals involved are very skilled and experienced as well as self starters. An example of where this style might work well would be a Construction Superintendent who has carpenters, electricians, plumbers and other highly skilled workers that are constructing a building.

There is a movement towards a balance between a highly directive style and minimally directive styles. In his book *The One Minute Manager Builds High Performing Teams,* Ken Blanchard refers to this style as the "Third Revolution"

- *Third Revolution* - empowers people and groups/teams, recognizing that "NO ONE OF US IS AS SMART AS ALL OF US". The leader only provides direction in assisting the team to develop an understanding of what their role is, what their task is, or when the team becomes bogged down. It is more of a coaching, facilitating and supportive role. The rest of the time the leader is a team member. This increases ownership of the project and allows team members to be creative. This style can be used in most leadership situations particularly where teams are involved. It will not be effective if an immediate response to an emergent situation is required.

Please understand that there is no black-and-white in being an effective leader – instead, there are many shades of gray. Your style will very much depend on your personality, your values and the circumstances of the task or decision to be made.

LEADERSHIP POWER BASES

Leadership power arises from the social position people hold (e.g., in a government, corporation, organization, etc.). and/or the knowledge and other skills they possess.

The seven Power Bases referred to by Leaders can be classed as Position Power or Personal Power.

- **Position Power bases** are Coercive, Legitimate, & Reward. These power bases refer mostly to the position you hold in the organization and are most effective with those who report directly to you. It is unlikely you can use these power bases to influence the behaviour of your boss or colleagues. Once a person accrues Position Power it is okay to use these to assert your right to manage. However continual reliance on these powers will most likely erode your influence over time.

Personal Power bases are Connection, Expert, Information, and Referent. They are based on who you are, rather than your position. Cultivating these bases of power

- provides the capacity to influence the behaviour of everyone – the people you supervise, as well as your bosses, friends, and colleagues. When you speak others listen. These bases are worth working on:
  - *Information* – it makes good sense to know what is going on in your own work area and in other areas within the business, company or organization.
  - *Connection* - build a network of contacts in and outside the organization (networking).
  - *Expert* - enhance your skills.
  - *Referent* - cultivate your image, confidence, communication skills and appearance.

Position Power Bases allow you to justify your right to manage, and Personal Power bases allow you to be seen as a leader. The goal is to make sure you use all seven power bases well so you can use them appropriately.

"THERE ARE TWO WAYS OF EXERTING ONE"S STRENGTH,
ONE IS PUSHING DOWN,
THE OTHER IS PULLING UP"
— Booker T. Washington

An example of using multiple power bases is that of a supervisor of staff who has the authority and right to expect and require others to carry out their orders. A good supervisor will balance this position power by having demonstrated their expertise and experience in the work they are asking to be done, and by their supportive and encouraging personality.

Another example is a basketball coach. The coach has the right to expect team members to follow the team rules and their orders at practices and games. They have the ability to punish if the player doesn't do that, by sitting them on the bench or kicking them off the team, or they may reward the player by providing playing opportunities. Coaches generally have expertise, knowledge and experience in basketball that assists players in wanting to both listen and perform for them. They can also be helpful in guiding and encouraging the players based on their ability and personalit

Position Power Bases

1. Coercive Power
- based totally on the leader's authority.
- forces compliance because failure to comply will lead to punishments such as undesirable work assignments, reprimands or even dismissal.
- some people successfully use intimidation to force compliance even if they don't have the ability to follow through.

2. Legitimate Power
- based on the legitimate social position held by the leader (e.g., judge, supervisor, etc.).
- in some cases, the higher the position, the more legitimate the power tends to be.
- persuades others because they feel the leader has the right to expect their suggestions/orders to be followed.

3. Reward Power
- based on the leader's ability to provide rewards for others.
- others will believe their compliance will lead to incentives.

Personal Power Bases

1. Connection Power
- based on the leader's connections inside or outside the organization.
- encourages compliance by others wanting to gain favour or avoid disfavor of those connections.

2. Expert Power
- based on the leader's perceived expertise, skill and knowledge.
- gains respect from others because of their skills and knowledge.

3. Information Power
- based on the leader's possession of, or access to, information that is thought to be of value to others.

- their access to information gives them power as others want access to the information or just want to be "in on things."

4. Referent Power
- based on the leader's personal traits.
- generally liked and respected because of their personality.
- influences people based on the respect they have earned.

With leadership there naturally comes some power - power to influence people to do things; to accomplish the goals of a business or organization. Truly successful leaders are able to use their power ethically, efficiently, and effectively by sharing it. Unfortunately some leaders abuse their power to influence people to do things they might not otherwise do and that has nothing to do with the business or organization's goals or purpose. Such use of power is unethical. Leaders who are in power positions have a responsibility to consider the impact their actions will have on others and on their organization as a whole.

ONE OF THE KEYS TO BEING A TRULY EFFECTIVE LEADER
IS HAVING STRONG ETHICAL VALUES AND
MAKING ALL YOUR DECISIONS AND CHOICES
BASED ON THOSE VALUES

In some respects, everyone has power—the power to either push forward or obstruct the goals of the group or organization. However, the effective use of power does not mean control. Power that is controlling can be damaging to a group or organization, especially when used to enhance the leader's own positions at the expense of what is best for everyone else.

ACTION STEP 3

Can you think of what power base, or bases, some of the leaders you know utilize? Here are a few persons you may wish to consider: parents, friends, teacher/professor, principal, coach, boss, or the mayor of your community. Can you think of any others?

CHARACTERISTICS OF EFFECTIVE LEADERS

In their book *The Leadership Challenge,* Jim Kouzes and Barry Posner say "what people most look for in a leader (a person they would be willing to follow) has been constant over time." This is based on regular surveys from six different continents, since 1987. Here are their top four, listed in order of priority:

- Honesty
- Forward-looking
- Inspirational
- Competent

Here are some additional leadership characteristics for you to consider:

Resourceful	Loyal	Fair
Supportive	Ethical	Reliable
Courageous	Determined	Charismatic
Enthusiastic	Decisive	Caring
Empathetic	Knowledgeable	Visionary
Facilitator	Communicator	Respectful
Initiative	Compassionate	Listener

This selection of traits is by no means complete. You will find that, as you encounter other effective leaders, you may be able to add even more words. Just be aware that all these characteristics are important and worth striving to attain.

Here is an acronym using the word **LEADERSHIP** to illustrate some of the qualities that an effective leader has:

L — **Listen:** with an open mind, wanting to hear what other people have to say.

E — **Empower:** delegating, encouraging and enabling other people to act.

A — **Awareness:** of what is happening, of trends and markets

D — **Desire:** shown by being enthusiastic, driven and determined to achieve the vision.

E — **Example:** being an example of the behavior you expect by serving as a role model for others

R — **Respect:** other members of the group, assisting and encouraging them to have confidence in their abilities.

S — **Self-esteem:** belief in oneself and leading with confidence.

H — **Heart:** care for other people, get to know them (and empathize with them, if appropriate)

I — **Initiative:** energy to make things happen.

P — **Patience:** slow to criticize, quick to praise.

Leadership can be both rewarding and frustrating. Rewarding as you see the progress you and/or your group are making towards achieving your goals, or frustrating as obstacles or distractions block your way. The following sections in this book should assist you in your journey and prepare you for dealing with those obstacles when they occur.

ACTION STEP 4

> *Look back and review the qualities or characteristics you listed earlier that you felt would enable you to become an effective leader. Do you still feel they are correct, or do you wish to add, change, or delete some of them*

ETHICS

"TRUST IS FRAGILE, LIKE A PIECE OF FINE CHINA, ONCE CRACKED IT IS NEVER THE SAME. PEOPLE'S TRUST IN BUSINESS AND THOSE WHO LEAD IT, IS TODAY CRACKING."
— Charles Hardy, the Harvard Business Review, December 2002

One of the keys to being a truly effective leader is having strong ethical values, and making all your decisions and choices based on those values. They are the standards of right and wrong that you have determined for yourself, and that will govern what you think, say or do. It also means taking full responsibility for your actions based on those ethical values.

Most Professions (e.g., medical, engineering), groups and organizations (e.g., churches, service clubs) and many businesses have a code of ethics they expect their members and staff to adhere to and follow. Rotary International, for example has a 4 Way Test. Most doctors take the Hippocratic Oath and many Churches teach the 10 Commandments.

Strong ethical values will earn you trust from the people you are leading or working with. Trust is an essential quality that creates a following for a leader and enables them to make a difference. It can't be demanded, it can only be earned. Remember if you want to gain trust from others you will have to demonstrate your ethical values by what you say and do. This is important in your personal, business or professional life.

Making ethical decisions is not always easy. The decisions you make may mean that the results you have anticipated do not materialize, so you are placed in a dilemma. For example, if one of your values is to always tell the truth, and you are questioned about an action of one of your friends: stating the truth will cause problems for them – and it may cost you a friendship. This may turn out to be a very difficult decision as you would have to live with the consequences, regardless of what your decision was - having to live with yourself for compromising your values, or, perhaps losing a friend. You may have read about journalists who are jailed because they refuse to name their source for a story. They have promised their source anonymity and to break the promise would limit future confidences.

TESTING ETHICS

Rotary International's 4-Way Test
Of the things we think, say or do:

Is it the truth?
Is it fair to all concerned?
Will it build goodwill and better friendships?
Will it be beneficial to all concerned?

You may find yourself in circumstances that are not comfortable and you're not sure what to do – after all, we are human. Here is a quick little 3-Way Test that you can use to help you decide what to do.

Will I get caught?
Will I get hurt?
Is it legal?

Or even simpler, when making a decision, ask yourself,

"What would my mother say if she knew?"

In his book ***The Contrarian's Approach to Leadership***, Steven B. Sample, President of the University of Southern California says that "Every leader must come to terms with his own moral beliefs and be held accountable in the end for the decisions he makes based on those beliefs". He goes on to say:"I am reminded here, of the words of a wise philosopher, my daughter Elizabeth; to the effect that moral leadership is less about what you're willing to live with – than what you're willing to die with."

Here are a few of examples of ethical values:
- I will demonstrate my ethical standards by example.
- I will lead with honesty and be guided by good values and strong moral principles.
- I will honor the differences in each person I am working with regardless of their gender, race or age.
- I will treat everyone with respect and value their contribution.
- I will consider who may suffer as a result of a decision I make and investigate reasonable alternatives to mitigate.

ACTION STEP 5

Start a list of ethical values you will ascribe to as a leader.
You may wish to head up your list with a title like "My 10 Ethical Values."
Don't worry if you can't think of 10 at this point –
You can add to your list as you continue your leadership journey.

As you develop your leadership skills over time, you will discover that trust is harder to come by than learning the other skills you need to be an effective leader. Trust can't be demanded, you have to earn it.

"WHEN THE BEST LEADER'S WORK IS DONE, THE PEOPLE WILL SHOUT, LOOK WHAT WE HAVE DONE OURSELVES"
— Lao Tzu, 6th/4th Century BCE

SECTION 2
DEFINING YOUR LEADERSHIP STYLE

"Who are you?" said the Caterpillar to Alice.

"I hardly know, Sir, just at present --- at least I know who I was when I got up this morning, but I think that I must have been changed several times since then."

"What do you mean by that?" said the Caterpillar sternly. "Explain yourself."

"I can't explain myself, I'm afraid, Sir," said Alice, "because I'm not myself, you see."

"I don't see," said the Caterpillar.

"I can't put it more clearly," Alice replied, very politely, "for I can't understand it myself..."

— Lewis Carroll, Alice in Wonderland

Now that you are aware of some of the qualities effective leaders possess, you need to focus on **who** you are. What are your values and beliefs? What are your strengths and weaknesses? What is your purpose in life, what do you want to be - and do? You will see exercises and comments later in this book that may help you answer these questions. You will probably find that, over time, your answers to these questions will change. In discovering yourself you will learn a great deal about relating to others.

This section of the book will help you make that journey of discovery.

WHO AM I?

One of the most important aspects of being an effective leader is to understand who you are and how you relate to others. Do you know who you are? Do really know who you are and what makes you tick? Do you know why you respond to people, things and situations the way you do?

Everything we do, say or feel is based on who we are at the time it happens. Whether we respond positively or negatively depends on who we have become. Knowing who we are helps us understand how we respond to people in a particular way, or why we react the way we do in certain situations. This can prevent embarrassing responses, by allowing us to prepare for those situations in advance, offering a greater sense of control and self-awareness. I must point out as well, that our emotions add a basis for how we respond, so we must be careful to **not** live by our emotions but, rather, by objective realities. In other words, to respond objectively rather than subjectively.

WHAT INFLUENCES WHO WE BECOME?

Many things influence who we become as we proceed on our life's journey; for example, our parents, friends, teachers, the media, various role models, and our family's ethnic background, social class, or religious beliefs. Noticeable physical handicaps or a difficulty in understanding the language may also be a major influence.

Many of us are bombarded with negative feedback from the time we are infants. Parents and families often give us misinformation, in an attempt to protect us from disappointments, failures, or exclusion by other people. This may be a result of influences on their own lives, or
may have come from their own fears and frustrations.

You may have heard some, or even all, of the following negative statements:
- You will never be able to do it
- You will never amount to anything
- You will grow up to be just like your dad/brother or mother/sister.

Joan Posivy, a well-known motivational speaker, says that when you are faced with negative comments, or when you are utilizing negative self-talk, you need to say **SWITCH!** to yourself. Then either move away from the negative influence or, if you are speaking negative self-talk, switch to positive self-talk —very wise advice!

ACTION STEP 6

Pick a day and record how you responded to something that happened that day—an event or something that someone said to you. Start with the first thing in the morning, then later that day, and then again before going to bed. If you responded negatively, think about how you could have turned the situation into a positive event.

LIMITING BELIEFS

Put-down phrases such as: *you are fat*, *you are ugly*, *you are stupid*, and similar words, can be devastating to anyone. The more we hear negative comments, the more conditioned we become to believe them.

The bad information we have been receiving may cause us to think and act accordingly. This is called **negative conditioning**. Unfortunately, if we are told these things repeatedly, over a long period of time, we often begin to impose limits on what we believe we are capable of
accomplishing. This is a self-imposed limitation; happily, it is reversible.

If you have had any experience with horses or dogs, you likely are already familiar with the concept of negative conditioning. Horses or dogs can be kept in a field by a single strand of wire, if it has an electrical current running through it. The horses lean against the fence and receive a shock. They are reluctant to try and lean against it again, particularly after being shocked more than once. The same is true with dogs. They wear a collar that will give them a shock if they come near the wire. You can actually turn the power off because they become conditioned to stay away (unless, of course, the horses accidentally lean against the fence or the dogs wander across the line and find that the power is off).

We can become like the horses and dogs if we allow ourselves to be conditioned by negative feedback. The good news is that if we lean against the fence, so to speak, we will find that the power is not on and we can move forward in our journey.

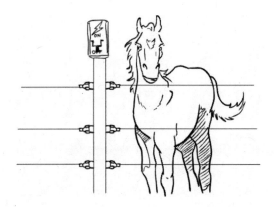

People who live by their own set of limiting beliefs may criticize you for setting goals, thinking about being a leader—or even reading this book.

Fortunately, many of us have parents, grandparents and friends who encourage us and tell us things like:

You can do it   We are so proud of you.

You are special   We love you

We often say to ourselves, "I should have done that," and regret missing out on that opportunity or situation. The following words, as seen on a poster, are good advice.

I will not SHOULD on myself today.

"The longer I live, the more I realize the impact of attitude on life. Attitude, to me, is more important than facts. It is more important than the past, than education, than money, than circumstances, than failure, than successes, than what other people think or say or do. It is more important than appearance, giftedness or skill.
It will make or break a company...a church...a home. The remarkable thing is we have a choice every day regarding the attitude we will embrace for that day. We cannot change our past...we cannot change the fact that people will act in a certain way. We cannot change the inevitable. The only thing we can do is play on the one string we have, and that is our attitude.
I am convinced that life is 10% what happens to me and 90% of how I react to it. And so it is with you...we are in charge of our attitudes."

— Charles R. Swindoll

ACTION STEP 7

> *We can change negative comments made to us into positive statements for ourselves, simply by turning them around.*
>
> *Sometimes it's about a habit we have fallen into—we can look at it objectively and say, "Is there something I can do about this?" For example, we might change the negative comment:*
>
> *"You spend too much time watching TV-—you won't pass your math test!" to, "I do watch a lot of TV. I need to change that. I will pass my test—and to make sure I do, I'll commit to studying for it for 30 minutes every day until I write it!"*
>
> *What negatives do you hear? Write them down and change them to positives.*

HOW DO I DISCOVER WHO I AM?

I encourage you to take an inventory of who you are, what has influenced you, and how you have responded to people and situations in your life. Be aware that outside influences, and other people's expectations can impact how you do things and how you react in certain situations. Be certain in your mind that it is you who is speaking and reacting, rather than you following someone else's voice.

A bonus in seeking to truly understand yourself is that you will be better able to understand others. You will discover that they also have a number of factors that influence them and how they respond to you, and to different situations as well. For example, you may have a friend who speaks loudly and sometimes seems to be aggressive in their manner, while another friend is quiet and sometimes reserved. This may be due to their respective personality types and/or learned behaviour from their home environment. While neither is wrong, these differences are the products of our upbringing and influence who we are.

If you are interested in exploring in more detail who and what has contributed to who you are, you may wish to spend some time talking with your parents and extended family. They can tell you about your family's history, where they are from (if from a different country or city), what their schooling was, what it was like growing up in their own family and in another time, and what they and/or their parents once did for a living. It is surprising how much you can learn about yourself from doing this and how much enjoyment your parents and relatives will have in telling you. This also will help improve your understanding of your family.

"REGARDLESS OF HOW OUR BACKGROUND AND CIRCUMSTANCES HAVE INFLUENCED WHO WE ARE WE ARE STILL RESPONSIBLE FOR WHO WE BECOME"
— Dave Douglas

ACTION STEP 8

> *Create your own self-inventory using these questions:*
> *What is my life all about?*
> *What do I believe in?*
> *What are my core values?*
> *Do my core values identify who I am?*
> *What do I do well?*
> *What do I need to improve?*
> *What fills me with a sense of wonder?*
> *What am I passionate about, and why?*

VALUES AND BELIEFS

I quite often refer to values and beliefs. They are an integral part of who you are and how you function. They filter in what you experience, read and hear, as well as how you respond to people, situations, and life in general. They should form the basis upon which you establish your personal mission statement and your goals. My interpretation of values and beliefs are as follows:

Beliefs are what your values are based on. They are statements, principles, or doctrines that we choose to accept as true (although they may not be). Beliefs are assumptions we make about ourselves, about others in the world and about how we expect things to be. It is placing confidence or trust in a person or thing. For example, I believe that when I step on the brakes my car will stop. I have placed my confidence in that belief although, if the brakes are poorly adjusted or worn out, that belief may suddenly be challenged.

Values are the worth or importance we assign to things and ideas. Values impact the way we perceive things to be or the way we think people should behave. They are about how we have learned things ought to be. Following my example of the brakes, my values might be the safety standards mandated for car construction, the quality of service I receive from our mechanic, and regularly scheduled preventative maintenance checks.

Here are more examples.

Belief: I believe in a democratic society.

Values: I value freedom of speech
I value the opportunity for self-determination
I value the opportunity to make choices within the laws.

Belief: I believe that family is the foundation of a strong society.

Values: I value the unconditional love that families share
I value the nurturing and modelling of parents
I value the interaction with my siblings.

While many additional values could be added under each of these examples, I have included only a few, to give you a basic understanding of my interpretation of the difference between beliefs and values. People often have difficulty defining the difference between beliefs and values because they are so closely related. As you will note, this is a very complex and academic subject to wrestle with. My advice is to not worry about trying to master the definitions. Instead, just identify things that are really important to you. Ask yourself questions like: *What do I really care about, and why? What kind of a person do I want to be, and why?* The clearer you are about what you value and believe the more effective you will be.

This exploration into your values and beliefs is for your benefit alone, to help you in your self-discovery and in developing your mission statement and goals.

"IT IS NOT WHAT WE GET. BUT WHO WE BECOME, WHAT WE CONTRIBUTE ... THAT GIVES MEANING TO OUR LIVES"

— Tony Robbins

ACTION STEP 9

Take some time now and make a list of things you believe in strongly and value greatly. Add to your list as you identify other ones, and refer to your list when developing your mission statement and goals.

TAKE TIME TO REFLECT

One thing many of us don't do particularly well is taking some time to be quiet and reflect on who we are, where we are going and how we will get there. If you can find a way to spend half an hour per day—or even if you only start with 15 minutes and work your way up to half an hour to do this—you will see a difference. These times of reflection are a great opportunity to get in touch with your life. They are a chance to review how things are going, for self-evaluation, and an opportunity to look into the future. It is also a great opportunity to take a break from the busyness of school, work and other activities that take so much of our time, to focus inward rather than being constantly distracted by external influences.

Time for reflection is one of the activities we have introduced to the young people who attend the Rotary Leadership Camps I am connected with. While it isn't easy for everyone to do, and we often face resistance (**I can't concentrate; there are too many distractions; I can't sit still**, etc.), after the camp, reflection time is one of the things we receive many letters about from youth telling us how important that time has become to them as they have gone on to university and/or pursued their careers.

Guidelines for Reflective Time

- set aside half an hour per day for reflection.
- try to use the same half hour each day, as it will then become part of your daily routine—something you will actually miss if you forget to do it.
- find a quiet spot where you are unlikely to be disturbed. It makes sense to use this spot each time so it becomes your personal area.
- ask your family and friends not to disturb you.
- turn off your cell phone, TV and computer; only listen to music if it won't distract you.

We spend most of our time living life and very little time learning from it. Devote your half hour to examining your inner self, your values, desires and accomplishments. Also, it is important to examine your mistakes so that you can learn from them.

Note: You may also consider walking, hiking or running during your reflective time. This will add an exercise component to your life and the opportunity to enjoy nature.

ACTION STEP 10

Reflect on these questions to get you started on your questions. Please note: don't do these all at once – this is reflective time, not a work assignment.

What did I do today that worked/didn't work? Why?
What would I do differently next time?
What do I really care about?
Did I do something valuable yesterday/today?
What guides me? Inspires me?
How do I feel about my behavior today?
Did I follow my goals?
What did I learn about my strengths?
What did I learn about my weaknesses?
What made me feel happy or sad yesterday?
What am I most afraid of?
What are the things that I value most?
How are my relationships with my friends?
How could I have handled a certain situation better?

JOURNALING

Some people like to journal their thoughts during this time. It may be something you wish to try.

Journaling is writing down what you are thinking about, how things are affecting you and what they mean to you. It can help you understand more clearly what you are thinking, especially when you are concerned or upset about something.

You are not writing a term paper or an essay for school; this is just for you. Avoid editing, analyzing, or criticizing the writing itself—simply put pen to paper and write down whatever comes out. Allow your deepest thoughts and feelings to flow. Review what you have written only when you have finished writing.

You may wish to begin keeping a Leadership Journal using a notebook or your computer. **Do not** put your journaling on Facebook or your blog—again, it is important that you keep your journaling just for yourself, so that you will not receive any feedback on it except your own.

One way to journal is to draw a line down the centre of a page and title the left column, **Things I did/learned today**, and the right column, **What it meant to me.**

Consider jotting down thoughts as they come to mind so that you won't lose them. After you have read what you have written, you may either wish to destroy your notes, or keep them in your journal so you can look back and see how you have evolved. It will also be a great source of history for you to review later in your life.

SUMMING IT ALL UP

Numerous factors, both negative and positive, can influence who we are. Many people have overcome negative influences and other handicaps to have happy and productive lives.

A great example of someone who overcame a severe physical handicap, and went on to lead a very productive and fulfilling life, is Rick Hansen. Rick grew up in Williams Lake, B.C. He was a carefree teenager who lived and breathed sports. At the age of 15, he hitchhiked home from a fishing trip. The truck he was riding in went out of control and crashed. As a result of injuries sustained in the crash the doctors told Rick he would never walk again. They were right.

Although he could no longer walk, Rick could still dream. He became an elite wheelchair athlete, winning 19 international wheelchair marathons, including 3 World Championships. He won 9 Pan American Wheelchair Games events (setting 9 records). He also competed for Canada in the Paralympic Games in 1980 and 1984, winning 6 medals (3 Gold, 2 Silver, 1 Bronze).

Rick Hansen was the first student with a physical disability to graduate in Physical Education from the University of British Columbia.

To find out more information about Rick, visit his web page at http://www.rickhansen.com/

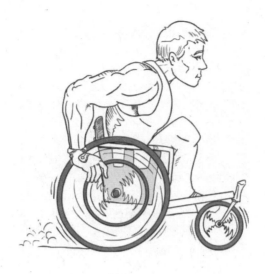

**"YOU HAVE TO BELIEVE IN YOURSELF WHEN NO
ONE ELSE DOES.
THAT'S WHAT MAKES YOU A WINNER".**
— Venus Williams

Remember this very important fact: regardless of how our background and circumstances have influenced who we are, we are still responsible for who we become!

Good luck on your voyage of self-discovery. You will not only be more powerful because of this knowledge (because knowledge is power), but it is my experience that you will be less likely to criticize or judge others. You will have learned that anyone can become a leader, and you also will have determined whether or not you wish to pursue being a leader rather than a follower. In the next section I outline how you can begin to develop your leadership skills.

**"SUCCESS IS NOT FINAL, FAILURE IS NOT FATAL:
IT IS THE COURAGE TO CONTINUE THAT COUNTS".**
— Winston Churchill

SECTION 3
DEVELOPING YOUR
LEADERSHIPSKILLS

"CONSIDER THIS POINT. THERE WOULD BE NO NEED FOR LEADERS
IF EVERYONE WAS A FOLLOWER – BUT FOLLOWERS NEED SOMEONE TO FOLLOW. SO LEADERS ARE ALWAYS NEEDED".

— Mavis Andrews

BY NOW YOU may be developing an idea of who you are and why you would like to be a leader. In this section of the book you will learn how you can develop your leadership skills.

In order to become a successful and effective leader you need to develop a number of skills. It is not enough to be popular or charismatic, or have a vision based on your values and beliefs. There are many things to learn, and it is a lifetime study if you want to be successful. You need to communicate your vision clearly and effectively to the people you are working with, and know how to encourage them to work with you to achieve the goals that will allow you to achieve your vision. You need to be a critical thinker and someone who can make timely decisions when required.

ACTION STEP 11

> *You may wish to stop at this point in your reading and, based on what you have read and thought about so far, consider whether or not you want to be a leader. Or would you rather be a follower? After all, following might be so much easier, safer and more comfortable. Write your thoughts about this in your journal.*

"LEARNING IS A TREASURE
THAT WILL FOLLOW ITS OWNER EVERYWHERE."
— Chinese Proverb

In this section, I have identified four skills for you to focus on:

- **Communication**—the ability to clearly and effectively communicate your vision to the people you are working with and to encourage them to work with you to achieve the goals that will enable you to achieve the vision.
- **Critical thinking**—the ability to look at all sides of a question or issue and to imagine and explore potential solutions.
- **Decision making**—the ability to make timely decisions when required.
- **Working with people/groups**—the ability to work with others, understanding their strengths and weaknesses, and how to help them become a productive team.

This section includes basic information on these important areas; however, these are only a few of the skills an effective leader needs, and each one could fill an entire book on its own. This section merely highlights the areas I feel are most important for potential future leaders. I hope you will continue to learn and seek more information on each of them, as well as other leadership skill sets that you find interesting.

As you grow into your leadership roles you will discover areas you need to learn more about in order to be more effective.

I firmly believe that once you stop learning and seeking ways to improve your leadership skills you stop being an effective leader.

Later in this section I will outline some of the ways you can continue to develop your skills.

EFFECTIVE COMMUNICATION SKILLS

Effective communication is a critical skill for a leader. As a leader you will spend a great deal of your time (some estimates say as much as 75%) in interpersonal situations. When problems occur in a group or organization it is often the result of poor communication.

There are many ways leaders communicate with their group, including:
- in general conversation; providing direct orders
- in writing, including memos, plans, reports, email and text messages
- by telephone, including calls and messages
- by fax
- through social media such as blogs, Face Book, Twitter, etc.

As a leader, it is essential that you ensure that any communication you make or receive is acknowledged and clearly understood. It is so easy to misunderstand or misinterpret information—unfortunately, that is what happens far too often. You will find that many people are not good communicators.

> *Note: Speaking without thinking about what you will say might place you in a situation where you regret saying something—just like hitting your send key on e-mail. Once that has happened the communication is gone and cannot be undone.*

Below are a few tips to help you ensure the communications you send or receive are clearly understood:

Clear Communication:
- Encourage the people with whom you communicate to feel comfortable about asking for clarification or further information if they are unclear about what you are saying. Make sure you do the same thing.
- Seek feedback to ensure your communication is clearly understood.
- Never assume the information you receive is correct until you check it out. It helps to know the person who is providing you with information and their track record for accuracy.

- Critical information should always be sent or received in writing, as memories are often short, and if information is passed on verbally from person to person it is often changed considerably by the time the last person receives it.
- Encourage people to listen and read carefully and focus on the communication they are receiving.

Communication entails being a good listener, understanding nonverbal cues and speaking clearly so you are understood. It has been said that "we have two ears and one mouth, so we should listen twice as much as we speak." Very good advice! If communication is to be effective, each person must feel good about themselves and the others, feel that the process is effective, and feel that their needs are met.

Here are some tips to assist you:
Listen
- Listening is **wanting to hear**.
- Don't try to think of responses while people are speaking.
- Provide feedback—nodding, smiling, eye contact, repeat statements to ensure you have heard correctly.
- Ask questions for clarification.
- Listen objectively, without judgement, until you hear the other person's point of view.
- Avoid multi-tasking, so you can receive the full impact of the speaker's comments.

Be aware of nonverbal cues
- People's body language can tell you how they are responding to what you are saying, or if they are paying attention.
- In our culture it is generally held that up to 60% of communication is nonverbal. By observing those cues, you can tell a great deal about whether people are listening to what you have to say and whether or not they agree with you.
- Eye contact is important in assessing where they are coming from with respect to communication.

Note: Nonverbal cues will vary from culture to culture. If you are meeting with someone of another ethnic background, try to learn about any differences beforehand.

Speaking
- Speak clearly, concisely, and at a level the person(s) you are speaking to will understand.
- Use plain language whenever possible. Avoid jargon (as specialized terminology or acronyms).
- Be natural; your normal persona works best.
- Practice as much as you can at getting your ideas across (many people practice speaking in front of a mirror—that way they can observe their body language and facial expressions at the same time).

Observe
- When speaking with someone, try to avoid being defensive.
- Don't make value judgement—just listen and observe.
- You don't have to agree with them—just try to understand where they are coming from.

Constructive Feedback
- Leaders need to provide constructive feedback; while it is not always a pleasant task, it is important.
- Many of us are afraid of offering constructive feedback because we are concerned how it might impact the person to whom we are talking.
- Leaders need to assist people to learn and improve—it's essential to the success of any group or organization.
- To avoid providing constructive feedback would be like sending someone on a hike to an area that is not familiar, without a map or a compass.

ACTION STEP 12

The next time you are communicating with someone, notice their body language and record your observations in your Action Guide.

Note their physical position (are they close or distant from you?), their arms (are they closed/open?), their facial expressions (smiling/frowning?) and head movement (nodding in agreement/shaking in disagreement). Are they maintaining eye contact with you?

As an effective communicator, you will develop a sharp awareness of what is taking place as you communicate with others. You will be analyzing where the speaker is coming from, listening in a non judgemental way, studying the person's body language and listening to the tone/inflection of their voice. This is a good habit to practice and you will find it very helpful when communicating with others.

"LEADERSHIP AND LEARNING ARE INDISPENSIBLE TO EACH OTHER"
— John F. Kennedy, 31st President of the United States

ACTION STEP 13

> *As a fun exercise, write down some observations in each of the areas I have noted above, the next few times you engage in a conversation with someone.*
>
> *Record your observations in your Action Guide and review them periodically. This will help you remember these communication techniques.*

CRITICAL THINKING

Critical thinking has been humorously defined as the art of thinking about your thinking while you are thinking in order to make your thinking better. Realistically, it is the ability to gather information, evaluate it and then make a decision based on the evidence.

Today, perhaps more than any other period in time, the ability to be an effective critical thinker is important. We are bombarded with so much information, often conflicting, that we have difficulty in knowing what or who to believe. The use of critical thinking skills can help you make appropriate judgements based on your values and beliefs.

Here are some suggestions to guide you in this process:
1. Clearly identify the area/topic you wish to explore
2. Gather information
3. Evaluate what you have found
4. Consider the alternatives
5. Select your position based on your values/beliefs—they can mediate the role that your information/knowledge has in influencing your judgement.

Let's look at the example of climate change. It is a topic intensely debated in many areas throughout the world: is there, in fact, global warming? And is it affecting our climate?

Applying the process outlined above you might wish to proceed as follows:

1. The **topic** — Is our climate changing?
2. **Research** this topic by seeking information in writing, or in person, from people such as environmental scientists and meteorologists—you will need to get more than one opinion, as scientists may not necessarily agree on the subject. In fact, it is advisable to seek out differing opinions so that you have varying views to support your analysis. A number of scientific papers have been written supporting both the pro and con points of view. Be aware of the legitimacy and authority of websites and other sources.
3. Next, **evaluate** the information you received. Who provided it? What were their possible biases? Was it fact or fiction? What evidence did they provide?
4. Then, **consider** the alternatives and identify some potential solutions. What are the pros and cons? Do you need more information?
5. Form a **conclusion**. This is not always in support of one side or the other—it may be somewhere in between. For example, in this situation your conclusion may be — that there is some evidence that our climate is changing.

- You may discover topics for which you are uncertain as to how to proceed, or are no

     You may discover topics for which you are uncertain as to how to proceed, or are not sure as to who to contact for suitable and factual information. This is an opportunity for you to utilize the knowledge and experience of a mentor, teacher or your parents to assist you.

     This process can be applied to any subject. If your opinion on a subject is different from a friend or someone else, use this same process. Try to understand the other person's point of view. List all the reasons their opinion could be valid, and then list the flaws in their argument. Analyze your position carefully to ensure that all your points are valid.

     Understanding all sides of a subject can be extremely helpful in making your case and in ensuring your points are valid.

     Many schools have debating tcams and if you have ever attended a formal debate you will understand the purpose of this type of thinking. These are the skills debaters use to be successful. You will be able to use them all through your life, if you learn how to apply them appropriately.

     I just recently read an excellent eBook entitled *Think Well & Prosper*, written by Steve Bareham, that provides a much more detailed and in depth approach to the art of critical thinking. If you wish to pursue more information on this subject Steve's web page is **www.summapublishing.net**

ACTION STEP 14

Is there a subject you wish to consider by using critical thinking?
Define your topic and follow the process outlined above.

DECISION MAKING

While critical thinking is a process of simply analyzing facts, decision making is a process of understanding what you want to accomplish. You make a list of options, determine the pros and cons of those options, and then select the best option for you.

Unfortunately, many people make decisions based on what others around them are doing or how they have dealt with similar situations in the past. They don't consider the consequences that may result. Peer pressure and mass media can influence your decisions; you need to be aware of that. Some people make decisions based on their feelings at the time—I am certain you have heard the term gut reaction. Others fear making decisions, thinking, *What if I am wrong?*

Take some time before making a decision to review your options and identify the pros and cons of each. Weigh them against your values and beliefs before you make your decision. This is a responsible way to ensure, as much as possible, that you are not making a mistake. If you have difficulty with a decision, you may wish to review your thoughts with your mentor, if you have chosen one. Mentoring is covered later in this section.

Don't be afraid to make mistakes, particularly if you learn from them. If you are not making mistakes, you are probably not challenging yourself.

Here is a little template you can use while making your decisions. I call it MY *WORD* ON THE SUBJECT:

> *W* → *what* do I want to accomplish?
> *O* → what are my *options*?
> *R* → *review* the pros and cons
> *D* → my *decision* is?

WORKING WITH PEOPLE/GROUPS

The dictionary defines a group as two or more individuals who influence each other through social interaction. This could be as simple as being on a date, or as complicated as working with a large group of people.

When you are working with a group, there are actions and forces that influence how the interaction takes place in the group. Here are just a few examples of these actions/forces that I have experienced in working with people and groups over the years:

Personal needs—these can be physical or emotional; such as room temperature, quality of seating, lack of tables for writing, meetings that run too long, too late, or without breaks. It could also be the need for recognition.

Hidden agendas—when a person or, if you are in a group setting, one or more individuals have other undisclosed plans or ideas. For example, they may have a favorite TV show they don't want to miss, or an arrangement to meet someone at a certain time, and the length of the meeting is causing them to miss it. They may be completely opposed to an item being discussed; it may even be something that contradicts their values/beliefs and so they may try to delay or sabotage a decision about it.

Differing perceptions—people see or understand things differently, that's just human nature. It is interesting to ask a police officer about this. When the police interview a number of witnesses to the same accident or crime, perceptions of the height, weight and clothing observed can vary dramatically in witness accounts.

Challenge to the leader—occasionally members of the group feel they can do a better job than the current leader, and a power struggle takes place.

ACTION STEP 15

> *You may have been on a date or attended some meetings of groups or organizations already. From your experience, can you identify some actions/forces you have witnessed taking place that make it difficult for the date or meeting to keep on task or to end with a satisfactory conclusion? Take a minute or two and write them down.*

Effective leaders understand that these types of actions/forces are always present, and they know how to handle them. They also realize that these actions/forces cannot just be turned off or on as they wish, and that they can be positive or negative—depending on the circumstances. However, these negative forces/actions, can be manipulated into something positive. For example, you can choose a better room, turn on the lights, open a window and acknowledge differing perceptions.

So how does a leader deal effectively with individuals or a group? Here are some basic things to consider:
- First, you need to understand who you are, and what are your values/beliefs, as well as your strengths/weaknesses. Refer back to what you learned in Section 2.

- Learn as much about the person or people in your group as you can. What are their values/beliefs and strengths/weaknesses? Each of us is unique and has a set of skills and attributes that no one else has. You will be able to utilize their strengths and provide support in areas where they are weak. And remember—the people in your team or group are your most important resources.
- If you are working in a group setting, make sure your group isn't so large that it can't be effective. Although you may have more input from a larger group, it may extend the time of your meetings considerably to get everyone's input.
- Make sure everyone is aware of, and clear about, the goal or task that the group is working on. Seek input to ensure everyone is on the same page.
- For meetings, have a written agenda to keep everyone on track. Send it out before any meetings so that members can obtain any information they may need. Seek clarification as you move along in the meeting, to ensure everyone is understanding and is in agreement.
- Summarize verbally, and then follow up with a written report. Clearly state any decisions that were made and who is responsible for any follow-up required.

*TAKE A MINUTE OUT OF YOUR DAY TO LOOK
INTO THE FACES OF THE PEOPLE WE (LEAD).
AND REALIZE THEY ARE OUR MOST IMPORTANT
RESOURCES*

— Ken Blanchard

MENTORING

A mentor is someone who, based on their experience, knowledge and training, guides and assists another person in a one-to-one relationship. They are like a coach,
providing information, encouragement and advice.

I have mentioned mentoring at various times in this book. Mentors can provide insight, support and encouragement, as well as useful knowledge gleaned from their own experience and perspective. I have been fortunate to have had a number of excellent mentors throughout my life and today I still enjoy adding new ones. I have also provided mentoring to a number of people and I enjoy that aspect as well.

Mentors can assist you in a variety of areas, depending on their expertise and your needs. Here is a brief overview of mentoring and how to locate your own mentor(s):

Personal development—they can assist you in making decisions relating to various situations or crises in your life.

Athletics—assist you with skill development, insight into various techniques relating to your sport or event, and by encouraging you.

Education—tutoring support, helping with study habits, suggestions on what courses to take to assist you in a career path.

Career—knowledge of various jobs/careers and what training is required.

Can you think of other areas?

Regardless of your age, mentors can provide considerable assistance and support. You may find you will have a variety of mentors over the years. You will outgrow some and add others as you pursue your dreams and establish your goals during your journey through life.

You need to be careful about who you select to be your mentor(s). Choose people you like and admire, or who have the skills you would like to obtain. Here are some qualities to look for in a mentor:

- a good listener
- provides positive feedback—dump the ones who are often negative
- encourages you
- sets a good example—you would like to be like them
- honest—will tell you how it is, not what you want to hear
- helps you through a problem but doesn't provide the answer
- has a network of contacts.

Don't be afraid to ask someone to be your mentor. Most often people are flattered to be considered. I suggest you say something like this: *Would you mind spending a few minutes with me one day? I would like to ask you about your job and the kind of qualifications I would need to succeed in your profession.* Or perhaps you could say something like: *Mr. Smith, you are a much respected person in our community. I would like to ask you to recommend someone to me that I could have as a mentor.*

You may be surprised that they will offer to mentor you themselves. But don't be discouraged if they don't offer or can't suggest someone else to contact—just keep asking people until you find one.

Note: According to Greek Mythology, Ulysses' son, Telemachus, was tutored and guided by Mentor (who was Minerva in disguise). It is generally believed that the word mentor has been used since that time to describe people who guide and tutor others.

Your school may be able to help you find a mentor. Many schools have mentoring programs where the mentors have been screened and trained to assist young people. The Internet has a number of online mentoring programs (E-Mentoring), particularly in the area of career assistance. However, be careful, and make sure it is a reputable service; it would be wise to check their references before participating or providing any personal data.

I believe the best mentors are those in your own community. It is easier to confirm their suitability and they will be much more accessible.

> *"IF YOU WANT TO BE SUCCESSFUL, FIND SOMEONE WHO HAS ACHIEVED THE RESULTS YOU WANT AND COPY WHAT THEY DO AND YOU WILL ACHIEVE THE SAME RESULTS"*
>
> — Tony Robbins

Note: There can be some risks involved in using mentors. If a new mentor is very negative and puts you down—you don't need that. Don't bother calling them again. If your new mentor has other ideas on his/her mind, or, after a while, wants to become more than a mentor to you—you don't need that, either. Always meet in a safe setting like a coffee shop, library or school to avoid inappropriate behavior.

ACTION STEP 16

Think about what part of your life would benefit by having a mentor to discuss things with. Think of people you might approach to provide you with mentoring.

SEEKING FURTHER LEADERSHIP SKILLS

As mentioned earlier in this section, becoming a truly effective leader is a lifelong study. You will encounter a number of people, situations and experiences over the years that will influence how you lead. This may force you to modify the way you handle situations, or enhance what you are already doing.

To assist you in preparing yourself for your leadership role, it is essential that you continually work on developing your leadership skills. Stephen R. Covey calls this *Sharpening the Saw*—in other words, unless carpenters make sure their saws are sharpened regularly they will have a difficult time in cutting through their material.

Here are several ways you can do this:

- **Books**—reading has always been a favorite activity of mine. There are a number of excellent books available on many aspects of leadership, written by people who became very successful leaders. Those books often detail what worked well, both for the author and others. The books can be general or specific; for example, a book may refer to overall leadership styles, or focus on specific aspects of leadership. If there is an area of your leadership skills (e.g., communication, planning, visioning, decision making, etc.) that you wish to improve, you should be able to find a book with helpful advice on that topic.

  Note: When you read books on leadership, make sure you consider and weigh what is being said in relation to your own values and beliefs.

- **Courses/programs**—attending leadership courses or programs gives you an opportunity to hear directly from someone with expertise and experience in the leadership topic they are presenting. It is also a great opportunity to interact with other leaders who may be attending, to gain further knowledge. Often, there will be an opportunity to ask specific questions, share your ideas and receive feedback.

- **Networking**—with the availability of the Internet and electronic devices, it is easy to connect and keep in touch with other people in similar leadership positions. They can be people you have met through workshops, in the community or online. I find it helpful to connect on a regular basis with people who hold positions similar to mine in each of the communities where I have lived. Also, many businesses and organizations have a parent body or association that, in addition to hosting an annual conference, may publish a regular newsletter or magazine featuring articles of common interest.

- **Mentors**—mentors can be very helpful in terms of sharing their experiences, or even just to listen. I really encourage you to seek a variety of mentors to assist you with different needs and challenges as you grow in your leadership role.

"IF WE DON"T CHANGE, WE DON"T GROW.
IF WE DON'T GROW, WE ARE NOT REALLY LIVING"
— Gail Sheehy

As you explore and learn about new leadership knowledge, skills and techniques, it is very important to ensure they fit with your beliefs and values and with your personal mission statement. Some of the new ideas that are meaningful to you may mean that you change or modify your beliefs, values, and thinking over time—that is part of your ongoing growth and personal development. I think it is important to focus on aspects of what you read or hear that mesh with who you are (your goals, values and beliefs). Utilize your critical thinking skills when selecting what to add to your tool box of skills.

Earlier, I mentioned how I have found reading to be beneficial. Here is an example that outlines some concepts I gleaned from reading. What I have included here illustrates how I selected some new concepts to add to my skill set that are based on my values and beliefs.

I read an excellent little book some time ago entitled **_Gung Ho_**, written by Ken Blanchard and Sheldon Bowles. It is based on a true story of how a young woman used metaphors to turn a failing factory into a success by fostering excellent morale in the workplace. The metaphors are easy to remember and can be used for any group, be it family, work or a community organization.

The three principles of the **_Gung Ho_** approach are based on animals that
are indigenous to many parts of the world. They are:

- **Spirit of the Squirrel**—the squirrel reminds us of worthwhile work and shared goals, as squirrels must collect nuts and food to store for their winter food supply or they won't survive. Also, if you have watched and listened to squirrels, you will note they chatter a lot (communication)—this reminds us that our goals for our family or organization must be shared regularly with all involved and constantly reviewed to ensure that they are current and achievable.
- **Way of the Beaver**—the beaver reminds us that everyone has a skill or gift they can share. If you have seen a program showing (or actually watched) beavers building their lodge, you will notice that they all work together. There isn't one beaver standing on top, providing direction, nor does another beaver remove a stick that another beaver has placed. They all know what they have to do and everyone pitches in to get it done.
- **Gift of the Goose**—the goose reminds us to encourage one another, cheering each other on. Whether they are in the air or on the ground, geese are constantly honking—encouraging each other. The goose is a great example to us. Imagine how your workers or colleagues would feel if they were constantly encouraged. Encouragement can be as simple as a

pat on the back, a word of praise in front of colleagues, or a written note of appreciation.

Gung Ho utilizes the acronym **TRUE**, to ensure that encouragement is meaningful:

$T \rightarrow$ Timely

$R \rightarrow$ Responsive

$U \rightarrow$ Unconditional

$E \rightarrow$ Enthusiastic

Gung Ho has a number of excellent ideas regarding leadership. I selected the two above for my leadership toolbox, as being consistent with my values and beliefs.

*"LEARNING IS LIKE ROWING UPSTREAM:
NOT TO ADVANCE IS TO DROP BACK."*
— Chinese Proverb

ACTION STEP 17

Can you think of ways you could help other people in understanding the skills and/or strengths they have to share?

SUMMARY

I have only included a glimpse of a few of the areas I that are important to consider as you develop your leadership skills. I cannot emphasize enough the need to make becoming an effective leader a lifelong study. Take advantage of every opportunity to learn about leadership, by reading, attending workshops, studying in school/university, working with mentors, or any other process you can find. **You won't be disappointed.**

As you continue your journey as a leader you will most certainly encounter issues or situations that you find difficult—don't hesitate to ask for assistance or find a course or book to read on the subject. Others may have faced or identified similar situations and found appropriate solutions. Here is a saying that has served me well over the years:

"LEARN FROM THE MISTAKES OF OTHERS LIFE IS TOO SHORT TO MAKE THEM ALL YOURSELF"
—Source Unknown

SECTION 4
WHERE ARE YOU GOING?

"WOULD YOU PLEASE TELL ME THE WAY I OUGHT TO GO FROM HERE?"

"THAT DEPENDS A GOOD DEAL ON WHERE YOU WANT TO GO," SAID THE CAT.

I DON'T MUCH CARE WHERE," SAID ALICE.

"THEN IT DOESN'T REALLY MATTER WHICH WAY YOU GO," SAID THE CAT.

"SO LONG AS I GET SOMEWHERE," ALICE ADDED.

"OH YOU'RE SURE TO DO THAT," SAID THE CAT, IF ONLY YOU WALK LONG ENOUGH."

— Lewis Carroll, Alice in Wonderland

UNLESS WE KNOW where we are going, there really isn't any purpose or direction to what we are doing in our travels through life. Unless we know where we want to go and what we want to be and do, we probably don't feel a sense of purpose, but just live day-to-day, paycheck to paycheck. Being purposeless is very much like riding a bike without handlebars—it just goes in circles, never really getting anywhere.

One of the things that limit us in our life journey is the inability to set effective goals. Often, this is the result of our attitude. In Section 2, *Determining Your Leadership Style*, you learned about negative conditioning and how that limits who we are and what we do. In this section, you will learn how to get to where you want to be.

Goal setting is like a map that helps you locate where you are going and shows you how to get through obstacles. It is like a target towards which you move. Setting goals helps you focus your time, energy and resources on doing the very best you can.

There is something almost mystical about a clearly defined and visualized goal, when you have developed a plan and set a deadline for reaching it. It becomes a picture in your brain; you get a burning desire to accomplish it and it won't let you go. This has happened to me many times. For example, when I was 16, I set a goal to purchase a car when I could afford to. It had to be a blue car and within a certain price range—I actually found the one I wanted one week before I reached my goal of getting the money I needed. This book is another example. I set a goal to write this book and it then was on my mind ever since. Every time I read a book, attended a training session, discussed leadership with people or prepared presentations for leadership seminars, I related the material to the writing I was doing. Setbacks or delays only heightened my desire to get it finished.

I am sure this has been the experience of many others as well. In fact, Thomas Edison, who invented the electric light bulb and patented 1,093 inventions, described failed attempts as not being **failures** but **results** (on how the invention he was working on wouldn't work).

Goals can be large or small, depending on where you are in your life, and at times you may not achieve exactly what you were striving for. Earlier, I mentioned Rick Hansen and the remarkable achievements he accomplished by goal setting. Here are a few more examples:

James Benson Irwin, a pilot, was in a very serious plane accident and both of his legs and his jaw were broken. He also sustained a serious brain injury which caused him to lose his memory. It took him two years of work with psychiatrists before he recovered enough to fly again. James applied to NASA to become an astronaut, and was rejected: he applied several more times and was rejected each time. Then, finally, in 1966, he was accepted and, in 1971, he became the 8th person to walk on the moon.

My grandson, Eric, wanted to have a cell phone when he was eleven. His wise parents said he could have cell phone when he had earned enough money to buy and maintain one. Having set a goal, Eric thought about how he might raise the necessary money. One day after school, he wrote letters offering his services to walk and exercise dogs. He delivered the letters to people in his neighbourhood, and received his first client almost immediately! As a result, he was able to purchase his cell phone.

   Terry Fox lost his right leg to cancer. In 1980, he embarked on a cross-Canada run called the Marathon of Hope, to raise money for cancer research. With his artificial leg and a "shuffle-and-hop" running style, he was able to run about 24 miles (approximately 39 kms)/day. He managed
to run 3,339 miles (about 5,374 kms) in 143 days, before the cancer spread to his lungs and he had to stop. Terry died a few months later, but his inspiration has left a legacy— annual Terry Fox runs in Canada and around the world have raised several hundred million dollars for cancer
research.

ACTION STEP 18

There are so many stories of people who have overcome adversity to make a difference. Can you think of someone in your community who has a similar story?

*"YOU CAN'T STOP A PERSON WHO WANTS
TO GO SOMEPLACE
OR HAVE SOMETHING BAD ENOUGH.
YOU CAN'T BEAT SOMEONE WHO WON'T BE BEATEN."*
- Dave Douglas

Of course, just because you set goals doesn't mean you will always achieve them. There will often be temporary roadblocks and setbacks. Even the most successful people face them. They are not defeated by setbacks—instead, all they do is intensify their desire and determination so as to find a way to successfully reach their goals. Dr. Randy Pausch, author of the book *The Last Lecture*, uses the term **brick walls**, instead of obstacles or setbacks. He says that the brick walls are there for a reason—they are not to keep us out; they are there to give us a chance to show how badly we want something. They are there to stop the people who don't want it badly enough.

When you overcome adversity you are stronger—you will ask how you can learn from it and continue to work toward your goal. You will begin to understand the inner strength that you have, and with that ability you are even more determined to carry on.

Every problem contains a gift—focus on the gift.

Here is an example of focusing on the gift. When teaching goal setting, I often ask the group, *What if you wanted to go outside to*

*do something and it started to rain. **What could be a gift in that?***
Here are some of the answers I received:
-   the rain will increase the water table
-   it helps the flowers, gardens and grasses grow
-   beautiful rainbows
-   cools the temperature in the summer heat
-   the smell after the rain
-   cleaning dust from the buildings, flowers, etc.
-   a chance to work inside.

What I am saying here is that you can't control Mother Nature, but you can control your thoughts about her. You can't control having to go to school, but you can control your thoughts about it—by developing friendships, learning new things, experiencing self-discovery, and so on.

ACTION STEP 19

If you are having a problem or a roadblock in your life, no matter how large or small, take some time now and see if you can analyze a gift in it that might be there for you.

Note: The Chinese symbol depicted here has often been interpreted as representingboth crisis and opportunity – indicating that a crisis is an opportunity waiting to happen

In my sessions on goal setting, I always ask why people don't set goals. Here are some of the most common answers that I received:

- I don't know which goal to pick
- I don't know if I am smart enough
- I don't think setting goals is really that important
- I don't know how
- I find it too difficult to do
- I haven't got time to do it
- I don't want people to laugh at me
- I am afraid I might fail.

It is interesting to note that many surveys regarding goal setting indicate that only about 3% of people surveyed write out their goals and set timelines to achieve them. In follow-up surveys, those 3% have higher achievement levels in almost all aspects of their lives than those who do
not write out their goals and set timelines.

I am pleased to say that, in recent years, when surveying the young people who attended leadership camps I have led, or been part of, more than 10% were actively participating in goal setting. I am sure that they will be very successful in accomplishing their goals—and you can be too.

**"I CANNOT ALWAYS CONTROL WHAT GOES ON OUTSIDE.
BUT I CAN ALWAYS CONTROL WHAT GOES ON INSIDE."**

— Wayne Dyer

Now that you can see the role that roadblocks can play in our lives, let's look at goal setting. I will discuss the first portion of the goal-setting process that I share with groups in leadership programs. In Section 5, I will focus on **how you get to where you are going**.

GOAL SETTING

Step #1—List Your Desires/Wishes/Wants

- These must be your own— too often we are influenced by outside factors and the expectations of others (parents, friends, teachers, etc.).
- They must be written down. I suggest a notebook or a file on your computer, so you can keep them in one place and refer back to them as often as you wish.
- Don't prioritize them at this point; simply brainstorm— just a flow of ideas.
- Don't limit yourself—our world and life is such a storehouse of activities. For example, you might wish to be an astronaut, swim with dolphins, play a professional sport, sing on the stage, or anything else you can imagine. Again, don't worry about prioritizing at this point.

"DREAM NO SMALL DREAMS FOR THEY HAVE NO POWER TO MOVE THE HEARTS OF MEN."
— Johann Wolfgang von Goethe

- Aim for writing down 100 goals. Impossible, you say? It is actually quite easy. Here are some areas you can consider in establishing your goals:

Education	Friends
Hobbies	Travel
Family	Career
Intellect	Spiritual
Finances	Nutrition
Emotional	
Health and Physical Fitness	

Even if you can identify only 2 goals in each of these areas, you would begin with 24. I am sure you will be able to add to the categories above, and probably find many subcategories under each, and easily reach 100. For example under hobbies you could have music (singing, playing an instrument), collecting items (stamps, coins), reading, etc.

If you are cannot list 100 goals right away, don't worry. You can add others over time, as you think of them. And don't stop at 100 if the ideas are still flowing.

ACTION STEP 20

Now, take some time and begin on your list of 100 goals (you may wish to call it My Wild Idea List). Use the categories outlined above and add any others you can think of. Try to identify subcategories under each of the main categories. For example under travel you might look at local, country and international.

Step #2—Review and Prioritize Your List
- Select goals that are most important to you.
- Must be based on your values/beliefs.
- Set short-term goals (I suggest 6 months, or less).
- Set long-term goals (anything over the short-term goal timeline).
- Include some major long-term goals that will make you stretch out of your comfort zone (out of reach, but not out of sight).
- Break your larger goals into smaller goals, like stairs (one step at a time). This will make it easier and less overwhelming.

Let's say that your long-term goal is to become a medical doctor specializing in a family practice, and you are currently in secondary school, or beginning your undergraduate studies at a college or university.

There are a number of things to consider:

prerequisite courses	undergraduate studies
universities that provide degree	grade point average required
availability of internships	when to apply
number of years it will take	scholarships available
overall cost estimate	

Obviously there is much to consider overall, but once it is broken into small steps it becomes much easier. For example,

- Step A could be arranging a meeting with the school or post-secondary school counsellor to determine what courses and undergrad studies are required.
- Step B could be analyzing the courses required and your ability and aptitude to handle them.
- Step C could be setting goals for the GPA you require in each of those courses

Continue until you have identified all areas of consideration. Then work on the steps in sequence until you achieve the end goal.

ACTION STEP 21

Choose one of your important long-term goals from your list and break it into manageable steps, so that you can take action on it one step at a time.

"WE COME THIS WAY BUT ONCE. WE CAN EITHER TIPTOE THROUGH LIFE AND HOPE WE GET TO DEATH WITHOUT BEING TOO BADLY BRUISED OR WE CAN LIVE A FULL COMPLETE LIFE ACHIEVING OUR GOALS AND REALIZING OUR WILDEST DREAMS."

— Bob Procter

MAINTAINING BALANCE

It is important to ensure that you keep your goals balanced. What I mean is this: if you have outlined a number of areas in your life to focus on, you should try to set, and work on, 1 or 2 goals in each area. If you don't, an area of your personal growth could be neglected. For example, if you focus all your attention each day, after school and on weekends, trying to
obtain part-time or regular work to make money, you won't have time for friends, studies, or your family.

The following illustration identifies some of the areas in which you may wish to establish goals, using the analogy of a wheel, to emphasize the need for balancing your goals. The wheel's center— the axle—is labeled **YOU**. It represents your core self, where you are in your life, what you have experienced and learned, and what your values and beliefs are. This will continue to expand as you experience and learn new things. Everything revolves around you.

Moving out from the center, the next portion represents your protective shield (the bearings in
the wheel), which covers the axle and allows the wheel to turn smoothly. This is your spiritual essence. It filters what you receive

(hear, read, learn, experience) and what you give out (say, do), based on your values and beliefs.

The spokes of the wheel radiate out from the protective shield and represent the areas of your life in which you are setting goals.

A BALANCED LIFE

This figure shows a wheel with balanced goals that will provide you with a smoother ride through life.

The next figure, shows a focus on two main goals—travel and finances—with much less attention paid to recreation, friends, career, education and family. This creates an imbalance and a bumpy ride.

That kind of imbalance usually ends up in problems. For example, let's say you focus only on making money and working as many hours as you can. You may not be successful with your studies, and lack time for friends or leisure hours. It could ultimately have a very negative impact on your health. Can you imagine going down the road in a vehicle with tires that looked like that? You will achieve a healthier, smoother journey through life if you keep balanced goals.

AN IMBALANCED LIFE

A wheel that will provide a bumpy road through life.

Step #3—Write It Out

- Be specific—simple sentences or phrases are best. For example, if you wish to lose weight, writing I want to lose weight is not specific enough. Your goal should be I will lose five pounds by (the day and month).
- State goals positively with *I will*—do not use *I have to* in your statement. Some people write goals as if they have already accomplished them; for example, **I passed my science exam with a score of 87%**.
- Believe you can achieve your goals—winners expect to win. Use positive self-talk and don't listen to negative voices. If you hear negative voices, say **SWITCH!** to yourself and start giving yourself affirmations such as, I can do it, I am smart, etc.
- Be realistic and set obtainable (reachable) goals that are compatible with your personal values and beliefs. For example, if you are still attending school, and working only a few hours a week, you are unlikely to reach a goal of making $100,000.00 in a year.

"WRITE IT DOWN. WRITTEN GOALS HAVE A WAY OF TRANSFORMING WISHES INTO WANTS; CAN'TS INTO CANS; DREAMS INTO PLANS; AND PLANS INTO REALITY. DON'T JUST THINK – INK IT!"
— Jim Rohn

ACTION STEP 22

Review your list of 100 goals that you started back in Step #1. Go through them carefully and identify your 3 most important goals.

Step #4—Be a Multi-Goal Setter, not a Multi-Tasker

- In Step #1, I encouraged you to set multiple goals—100, if you recall. I believe it is extremely important to have as many goals as you can and make sure you have balanced your approach, as outlined in Step #2.

Note: as you are working on your goals, I recommend that you focus your action plans one step at a time. If you try to undertake too many steps, or too many goals, all at once, you will get bogged down, become frustrated, and not experience the success you should.

SUMMARY

During your journey through life you will experience constant change. You will find that your goals may shift, or even change completely, as you discover more about yourself and the many new opportunities that life will bring you. The key is to be flexible, while making sure that whatever you choose is consistent with your values and beliefs. Please remember to make your goals something that you really want, not something that merely sounds good, or that someone else has decided for you.

"YOU MUST HAVE LONG TERM GOALS TO KEEP YOU FROM BEING FRUSTRATED BY SHORT TERM FAILURES."
— Charles C. Noble

SECTION 5
HOW DO YOU GET THERE?

ONCE YOU HAVE established your goals (see Steps 1 to 4 in Section 4), they won't be anything to you other than a wish list, unless you do something about going after them. The next points are the action parts of the process I use and teach. At the end of these points I have included information on action planning, visualization, guided imagery and developing your own personal mission statement.

Step #5—Establish Strategies

- Develop action plans: write out the steps you can take to accomplish your goal. Later in this section you will find a detailed overview on developing action plans.
- Your goals and priorities must be congruent and reflective of who you are. That means you might have to adjust some aspects of your personality; for example, you might be shy but your goal includes public speaking. Using the goal of becoming a medical doctor(outlined in Step #2) as an example, if you require several science courses with a high GPA but you detest studying and would rather watch television, you are unlikely to reach your goal. If the goal is really important, you would have to change your study habits.
- Use positive self-talk. If you think about it, we are continually talking in our minds. Henry Ford, founder of the Ford Motor Co., said, *If you think you can do a thing, or you think you can't do a thing—you're right.*
- Work at eliminating *I should*. Instead, focus on *I want* and *I will*.
- Challenge yourself to accomplish your goals.
- Establish a reward for yourself on completing a goal. It may give you an incentive to go for it. Your reward can be as simple as going to a movie, or as exciting as taking a trip to Europe or Asia.

Step #6—Set a Time Limit
- Time limits are a critical component of goal setting and one that most people omit. This forces you to take action. Make sure you are specific, include an exact time and or date.
- Post your goal—with its **timeline**—where you can see it regularly (on your mirror, door, computer, etc.) so you are constantly reminded of it.

Step #7—Share your Goals
- Share with a friend, family member, mentor, or someone else you can trust, who will support and encourage you as you move forward. They can also act as a conscience for you as, hopefully, each time they see you they will ask you how you are proceeding. However, you may find you have some personal goals you won't want to share with others, and that is okay.
- Don't share your goals with people who say negative things like *you'll never do it*, *you are crazy* or *what a dumb goal*. When we listen to those types of people we become susceptible to their negative influence, and may either fail or experience more difficulty in achieving our goals.

When you fall into negative thoughts, remember to SWITCH! to positive ones.

Step #8— Visualize
- Visualization is a powerful tool in helping you to accomplish goals. There are a variety of visualization techniques, from simply closing your eyes and thinking, to a more complex guided imagery session that allows you to picture completing your goal successfully. The object of visualization is to picture yourself where you are when you achieve your goal: what you are wearing, who is with you, the sounds that you hear (perhaps clapping for your accomplishment), any smells, etc.

- Athletes utilize visualization to a great extent and with much success. You have probably seen an athlete on TV or at a sporting event going through their routine or event in their mind before they participate.
- Some people like to draw or cut out pictures of the goal they wish to accomplish and display it in a place where they may see it regularly. For example, if one of your goals was to buy a new car, you would research what model and color you wanted and then draw it, or paste a picture of it on a sheet of paper, and put it on the door of your room. That is also a form of visualization.

- I suggest that you use your reflective time (as outlined in Section 2) to actively engage in this process, so that you are not disturbed while visualizing.
- Later in this section there is a more detailed explanation of these visualization techniques.

Step #9—Record Your Progress
- Make a checklist of your goals and all the parts of them that need to be accomplished so that you can chart your progress. This can give you a boost and keep you focused. For example, if you need to complete 10 things to accomplish your goal and you get stuck on number 7, you can look at your checklist and see that you have already completed 6 of the steps and are over halfway there.

- It is like celebrating your score in a game. If you have accomplished 6 steps, you might write 6! next to your written goals. It works for businesses; they celebrate scores by publishing their targets and results—with great effect. Why wouldn't the same method work for you?
- Build on your successes. Success breeds success and gives you the encouragement and confidence to carry on.

Step #10—Go For It
- The first two letters in the word **Goal** are *Go!*
- **Action** versus **dreaming** is the key.
- Life is not easy—we don't come with an instruction manual, so don't give up. Like any other skill, goal setting skills are developed by practice. If you establish a pattern of working towards your goals it becomes a positive habit that will serve you well.
- Years ago, as a teen, I learned these 10 small but very powerful words:

IF IT IS TO BE
IT IS UP TO ME

No one else can do it for you.
"A JOURNEY OF A THOUSAND LEAGUES
BEGINS WITH A SINGLE STEP"
— Chinese Proverb

Step #11—Assess/Amend/Add/Delete

- I recommend setting a time monthly, or at least twice per year, to review your progress.
- This is an important step that will remind you of your commitments and where you are in relation to the deadlines you have set.
- You can assess whether or not you need to change, amend or delete any of your goals.
- This is also a good time to add any new ones to your list.

- For each new goal, use the process outlined above to assist you in accomplishing them.

Who Dares—Wins

My friend Andy was a co-leader of an overland expedition from South Africa to England in early 1955. He became very ill in Benghazi Libya. No medical facilities were available, so his friends placed him in the protection of an Arab animal enclosure to get him out of the sun. Scratched on the mud wall were the words *Who Dares—Wins.*

Andy adopted that motto and it has guided him in all the important decisions throughout his life. When Andy was 21, he set a goal to travel to 100 countries. As a guideline, he would stay in the capital of each and spend a minimum of one week visiting the main tourist attractions. It was a daunting task, considering travel costs, political unrest, conflicts and so on.

With his motto, **Who Dares—Wins**, and utilizing his leadership skills, he has already visited 131. A remarkable accomplishment!

"IN THE LONG RUN MEN ONLY HIT WHAT THEY AIM AT: THEREFORE ALTHOUGH THEY MAY FAIL IMMEDIATELY, THEY HAD BETTER AIM AT SOMETHING HIGH".

— Thoreau

SMART GOALS

You may find it effective to measure your goals by using the acronym **SMART** which asks for answers to the question, are my goals **specific, meaningful and measurable, achievable or attainable, realistic** and **timelined?** For example, if one of your goals is to buy a new car, you would ask for answers to the following:

> **S** → **specific**: you can't state your goal is to own a car. You need to make your goal more specific and include year, make, model, color, etc.
>
> **M** → **meaningful and measurable**: you would ask yourself how much you need to save, if it is a car that will serve your needs, if it is something you need at this point in your life?
>
> **A** → **achievable or attainable**: you would ask yourself if the budget you set for the car is attainable within the timelines you have established.
>
> **R** → **realistic**—is it feasible that you can achieve it? For example, if the car costs $20,000 and you have a part-time job where you only earn $100/week, it is unlikely you will be able to do it.
>
> **T** → **timelined**—set a specific date for completion. This is critical.

Smarter Goals

Wayne Hully, president of Canadian Effective Schools and The North Star Centre, is a highly sought after as a speaker, presenter and facilitator. He likes to add ER to the word Smart to make the acronym read Smarter. The ER stands for extra reach—challenging the people he is teaching to seek greater achievements.

Many people find it helpful to post their goals where they can see them on a daily basis. A place like a mirror in your bedroom, the inside of your bedroom door or on top of your dresser works really well. Others have goals displayed on their computer and refer to them when preparing daily, or weekly, *to do* lists. If you make *to do* lists, ask yourself, does this move me closer to achieving my goals?

ACTION PLANNING

Once you have developed your goals and set fixed timelines to achieve them, you need to develop action plans. This process helps you work out the most effective and efficient way to reach your goal. Action plans keep you on track and help you focus your energy. The process should help you identify all the factors you will have to consider and everything you will need in order to accomplish each goal.

Here are five steps to assist you in action planning. Use the same process for each of your goals:

Create Your Action Plan

Step A—Write down your top goal that you wish to achieve. Remember—your goal must be positively stated and specific. If it is a major goal, it helps to break it into small pieces and develop action plans for each piece. Think of your goals like stairs, climbing one step at a time to achieve them. If you have a long flight of stairs at home or school you will know that it is very difficult to go from the bottom of the stairs to the top in one leap.

Step B—List all the steps you need to follow to achieve your goal. These must be clearly defined—like developing a map for a road trip, where you will need to know the distance between stops, accommodation, food, money required and so on.

Step C—Identify when you will complete each step by using a time and date. A concrete timetable is a must as it forces action.

Step D—List any help you will need, and don't hesitate ask for assistance. Asking for help is realizing that no one can possibly know everything. It is a sign that you have high self-confidence. Look for someone who is already doing what you want to do—they may be very kind and encouraging, as they have most likely gone through many of the steps you will face. You may wish to refer back to the information on mentoring in Section 3.

Step E—List any other resources you may require such as money, books and information.

On the next page is a sample planning matrix you could use to list your goals and examples of the steps for this process:

Goal: *To travel to Europe.*

Action Plan

	Action Required	Assistance Required	Resources Needed	Completion Date	Done
1	Determine Destination	Talk to others who have been	Travel guides Maps	Feb. 4th	yes
2	Places to visit	Talk to others	Travel guides Books	Feb. 18th	yes
3	Travel Method	Travel Agent	Phone, names Of Agents	Feb. 24th	
4	Date of Travel	Travel Agent	Grad date? Best Dates re cost	Feb. 28th	
5	Travel Partner y/n?	Talk with friends		Mar. 5th	
6	Determine Cost	Travel Agent	Job/other funding	Mar. 10th	
7	Set a Budget	Confirm with Agent		Mar. 20th	
8					
9					

Note: Research could mean checking the internet, reading travel blogs, consulting a Travel Agent or discussing with friends or family that have already travelled to Europe.

Date Reached: _____

AS YOU BEGIN TO TAKE ACTION TOWARD FULFILLMENT OF YOUR GOALS AND DREAMS, YOU MUST REALIZE THAT NOT EVERY ACTION WILL WORK. MAKING MISTAKES, GETTING IT ALMOST RIGHT AND EXPERIMENTING TO SEE WHAT HAPPENS ARE ALL PART OF THE PROCESS OF EVENTUALLY GETTING IT RIGHT."
— Jack Canfield

ACTION STEP 23

Pick a typical day in your week and review what took place. Ask yourself:
Have my actions been consistent with my goals?
Am I making progress in my goals?
What is holding me back from reaching my goals?
What help do I need in reaching my goals?

When you have clearly defined and visualized your goals, developed a plan and set deadlines for achieving them, they become a picture in your mind and won't let you go. That picture forces you to act—**to go for your goals.**

The big advantage in writing all this down is that you can record your successes. If you become bogged down, you are able to look back and see what you have already accomplished, and become encouraged to carry on.

You may find that, regardless of how well you thought out your plan, you may have overlooked some aspect or obstacle that gets in your way. Don't be discouraged; just develop a new action plan to help you work your way around, over, under, or through the problem.

VISUALIZATION

Whether or not we realize it, everyone visualizes. You may visualize clear or fuzzy pictures, or you may even "see" them just in thought. Unfortunately, many people only visualize negative results, which could become a bad habit.

Many successful people, whether in business, professions, athletics, school or university, use visualization techniques as a tool to achieve their goals and consciously direct where they are going in their lives. You can do this too; it just takes practice. If you choose, it can become part of your reflective time.

In visualizing a goal you need to place yourself fully in the environment you would be in, as if you have already achieved your goal.

ACTION STEP 24

For example, let's say that one of your goals is to graduate from high school or university (or be honored in a similar ceremony).

Close your eyes and imagine the ceremony. Look around you—
what do you see?
Where is it being held—gym, auditorium, or some other location?
Who do you see with you—friends, classmates, teachers?
Are there decorations?
What are you and your friends wearing?
What noises can you hear—talking, music, cheering?
Are the people happy?
Are the grads sitting in a special place?
Is the school or university band there? Are you in the band?
Are your parents or grandparents there? Where are they seated?
Can you see yourself crossing the stage to receive your diploma?
Who is presenting it to you?
What are your emotions—happy, sad, apprehensive?

These are just a few of the sights, feelings and sounds you may experience. You may think of many others. Record your visualization. Revisit it periodically and note how you feel.

This process can be used for all of your goals. Once you have visualized accomplishing your goal a few times, the visualization really becomes part of you; as you read in Section 2, it becomes part of your subconscious mind.

Visualization has become an integral part of the sports world. It is used before and during games, events and even in practices. You can actually notice athletes— gymnasts, track and field participants, field goal kickers, ski racers, golfers, basketball players shooting foul shots, to mention just a few—using this technique just before they compete, kick or shoot. Watch for their heads, arms and legs moving the next time you watch a sporting event. If it works for athletes why wouldn't it work for you?

ACTION STEP 25

While the visualization questions are fresh in your mind, do another visualization based on your top priority goal. Go through the same steps as in the previous visualization—and remember to revisit it periodically.

"IT'S NOT THE WILL TO WIN THAT MATTERS –
EVERYONE HAS THAT.
IT'S THE WILL TO PREPARE TO WIN THAT MATTERS."
— Paul "Bear" Bryant, college football coach

GUIDED IMAGERY

If you have trouble visualizing on your own you may wish to try guided imagery. This technique can assist you in visualizing your goals, particularly if you have difficulty doing so on your own. As the name implies, there is a need for a guide, or facilitator, to lead the process. You can find prepared tapes, MP3s, CDs and books of scripts at your favorite bookstore or online by searching for *guided imagery*. However, it is just as easy for you create your own guided imagery recordings. I will explain how in a moment.

Guided imagery allows you to create a familiar, safe and controlled environment in which to explore and sense the feeling of achieving your goal. You use suggested mental images to explore the achievement of your goal. It is not difficult, and you can use this process every day. For example, if someone says to you, **would you like some chocolate ice cream?** you can imagine what it tastes like even before taking a mouthful. Or if someone says to you, **let's go skiing**, you can visualize your skis, the hill, the lift, and other aspects of the trip. You can recall what your bedroom looks like; visualize your favorite movie star and friends, and what you plan to wear tomorrow. Practice every day. Focus on achieving your goal. Remember—visualization may be a clear image, a fuzzy image, or just a thought.

Make Your Own Guided Imagery Recording
- you will need a way to record your voice.
- select relaxing music for background; it should not be too loud or it will be distracting.
- write out a list of questions or prompts relating to the accomplishment of your goal; you can use the questions listed above as a guide.
- be specific in your questions and prompts; focus on successfully completing your goal.
- it is important take time to relax before beginning your visualization recording; breathing or stretching exercises can be helpful.
- also to help you relax, play your background music for several minutes before you start reading your script.
- remember to keep everything in a positive tone; speak softly, but clearly.
- dictate your questions and prompts slowly and distinctly, leaving enough time in between to allow you to visualize; I suggest 15 to 20 seconds—see what works best for you.
- when you have completed reading your questions and prompts, let the music play for a while longer so that when you have completed your visualization, you can take time to enjoy the experience.
- review the recording; if you are not happy with it, do it over—practice makes perfect; you will find that each time you prepare a recording it will become easier.
- make a separate recording for each of your goals.

Good luck with creating your own guided imagery!

YOUR PERSONAL MISSION STATEMENT

Your personal mission statement will include what you wish to accomplish and contribute in your life, and who you would like to be. It will be based on your values and beliefs, and also the strengths and qualities you wish to develop. It becomes your personal constitution—the basis by which you consider and evaluate how you pursue your life.

Stephen R. Covey's book *First Things First*, is about managing your time, but he introduces the use of a personal mission statement as an important principle. He refers to developing a mission statement as connecting with your own unique purpose and the profound satisfaction that comes in fulfilling it. If you live by what is really important to you, you will manage your time and activities towards accomplishing your goals much better.

When preparing your personal mission statement it is helpful to ask yourself questions about your life, beliefs, core values, goals and actions.

"THE SECRET OF GETTING AHEAD IS GETTING STARTED. THE SECRET OF GETTING STARTED IS BREAKING YOUR COMPLEX, OVERWHELMING TASKS INTO SMALL MANAGEABLE TASKS, THEN STARTING ON THE FIRST ONE."
— Mark Twain

ACTION STEP 26

Prepare for writing your personal mission statement by asking yourself:
What is my life all about?
What do I believe in?

> *What are my core values?*
> *Do they identify who I am?*
> *Will the goals that I have developed help me reach my mission?*
> *What am I actively doing to accomplish my goals?*

Organize Your Thoughts

This outline will help you organize your thoughts when developing your personal mission statement:

1. Identify successes you have already accomplished. These can be at home, school, work, in your community. See if there is a common theme(s) to your examples and write them down.
2. Identify core values that identify who you are and what your priorities are. Narrow the list down to the ones most important to you.
3. Identify any contributions you have made that have made a difference to your:
   - family
   - friends
   - school
   - employer
   - fellow workers
   - community
   - the world in general.

Also, list ways you could make a difference in those areas, in an ideal situation.

4. Review the goals you have developed in relation to your priorities.
5. Develop a draft of your personal mission statement.

ACTION STEP 27

Using your successes, core values and contributions draft your own personal mission statement. Remember to: Keep it simple, clear and brief; try to keep it to 4 or 5 sentences maximum.

State it in positive terms—what you want to do and become— never include any negative statements

This is your guide in your day to day actions and decisions—refer to it as you develop goals and make decisions.

Review your draft mission statement in relation to the questions identified above.

- does it answer the questions in Action Step 26?
- does it say what you wish to accomplish and contribute?
- is it based on you own values and beliefs?

Rewrite your mission statement until you feel comfortable with it. Creating a personal mission statement is not something you do overnight. It takes careful thought and reviewing who you are and who you want to be. It may take you several weeks or months and many drafts to finalize it. If you pursue a quiet time, as suggested earlier, that will be a good opportunity to reflect and consider your personal mission statement.

Your mission statement is not static—it will change as you journey through life. As you develop knowledge and experience new things, your beliefs, values and goals will no doubt change. It is essential that you review it, at least annually, and modify it as needed.

"OUR LIVES BEGIN TO END THE DAY
WE BECOME SILENT ABOUT THINGS THAT MATTER."
— Martin Luther King Jr.

One way to consider beginning your personal mission statement is to create a chart like this one and fill in the blanks.

GOALS I WANT TO ACHIEVE	CONTRIBUTIONS I WANT TO MAKE	THINGS I WANT TO HELP OTHERS TO DO	QUALITIES I WANT TO BE REMEMBERED FOR

Then fill in a statement like the following:

I want to achieve _____[your goals here] because I want to contribute more _____ [contributions you wish to make] to the world and help others _____ [things you want to help them achieve]. By doing this, I hope I will be remembered as a person who was _____
[things you wish to be remembered for].

"YOU MUST BE THE CHANGE
YOU SEE IN THE WORLD."
— Mahatma Gandhi

Here are two examples of other kinds of personal mission statements that I have read:

My desire is to be healthy, fit and energetic, so that I can enjoy life to the fullest and have the energy to pursue all my goals. I will accomplish this by regular exercise, nutritious diet and eliminating negative habits that affect my life.

To graduate from school with a high academic standing so that I can pursue my goal of attending university, to become a lawyer. I will do this by focusing on my studies, completing my assignments on time and leading a healthy energetic life.

Here are three sample sentences with spaces for you to fill in the blanks, and things to consider, to assist you as you start writing your personal mission statement:

To _____ [what you want to accomplish or be in your life] so that _____ [reason why you want to do that]. I will accomplish this by _____
_____ [what goals and actions you will take to accomplish that].

My purpose is _____ [what you wish to do or be in your life] because I value ____
_____ [why it is important to you to do that]. I will _____ [how you will do that].

To develop strong leadership qualities _____ [list 2 or 3 leadership characteristics] that I respect in _____ [name of a leader/ person you admire] so that _____[reason you selected those characteristics].

"DECIDE UPON YOUR MAJOR DEFINITE PURPOSE IN LIFE
AND THEN ORGANIZE YOUR ACTIVITIES AROUND IT."
— Brian Tracy

This is my personal mission statement that helped me focus on writing this book:

My purpose is to share with young people what I have learned and experienced in my life with a focus on leadership and what it takes to be an effective leader. I will do this by mentoring when requested, developing and presenting leadership programs and writing a book on the subject.

SUMMARY

I encourage you to begin writing your personal mission statement. You may find it difficult to get it just the way you want it on your first try, but don't give up. Each time you work at it you will find it easier—and it will continue to change as you grow in knowledge and experience.

Remember, it is your own mission statement. You are not writing it to impress anyone else—as long as it is clear to you, it is good.

"FOR EVERY FAILURE THERE'S AN ALTERNATIVE COURSE OF ACTION.
YOU JUST HAVE TO FIND IT. WHEN YOU COME TO A ROADBLOCK, TAKE A DETOUR."
— Mary Kay Ash

SECTION 6
CLOSING WORDS

THE SKY IS THE LIMIT

CONGRATULATIONS! YOU HAVE worked your way through this book. I sincerely hope you found it worthwhile. You now possess basic information on what leadership is all about and a sense of whether or not you want to be a leader. In fact, you probably now have more knowledge of basic leadership skills, and what is entailed in being a leader, than most other teens and many adults.

I hope you will use these skills and continue to build on them as you make your journey through life. It is a lifelong challenge if you want to be a really successful leader.

Although being a leader can be difficult and frustrating at times, in my experience, the successes have always surpassed the difficulties. There is nothing more satisfying to a leader than to have a project successfully completed, with all participants satisfied and proud of their accomplishments.

If the skills and knowledge in this book have been helpful to you, I would love to hear your stories. If you have any questions, or require any clarification, I would be happy to assist you with those as well. My website is www.leadingtheway-book.com.

With your goals defined, your action plans thought out, and your personal mission statement as your guide—there is no telling what the future may bring for you!

"ACT THE WAY YOU'D LIKE TO BE
AND SOON YOU'LL BE THE WAY YOU ACT"
— Leonard Cohen

DEDICATION

This book is dedicated to my grandsons, Jon and Eric Douglas, and granddaughter Hailey Haddow who are already demonstrating excellent leadership skills, and to my newest grandson, Damon Haddow, who I am certain will do the same.

This book is also dedicated to the many youth I have worked with over the years as a team coach, coordinator of Youth Programs, teacher, mentor, or in any other capacity. I thank you for your confidence in me—and for all that you have taught me in return.

ACKNOWLEDGMENTS

Without the significant contributions and encouragement from my family, and many friends, mentors and colleagues, this book would certainly not exist.

I am particularly indebted to a number of critical readers, who invested significant hours in reading drafts of the manuscript, providing suggestions and additions that significantly improved the original work as well as encouragement; continually reinforcing my faith in the potential of the book. They are, in alphabetical order: Allison, Mr. Kas Angelski, Dr. Jennifer Chapman, Mr. Mark Douglas, Mr. Gary Gumley, Mr.Tom Hierck, Cindy Ngan, Ms. Christy Poirier, Dr. Tom Ristamaki, Samantha, Ms. Stacey Semenoff, Tyler Vanderheyden.

To my children—you have brought me years of enjoyment as I have watched you grow and develop your leadership skills. I hope my example has been of some assistance to you.

To all the young adults who have attended the Rotary Leadership Camp (RYLA) in the past 29 years, thank you for sharing part of you with me, and allowing me the opportunity to share much of what is in this book with you. You have always given me great hope for the future as I
know you will provide the leadership needed for our communities, our countries and the world.

A special thanks to all the RYLA staff and guest presenters with whom I have worked in the RYLA program; in addition to your friendship and encouragement, you have taught me a great deal. I am certain you will see glimpses of each of you in this book.

I have been blessed with a number of mentors and great friends over the years in my work and personal life. You have made a significant difference in my life and continue to do so.

A special thank you to Kirsten Anderson, Teen Services Librarian, Greater Victoria Public Library, who patiently answered many questions, provided encouragement and arranged for her Advance Reader Group to review a draft of my manuscript. They provided excellent suggestions.

The cover design was created by Nick Johnson of Hey You Media. Illustrations were created by Greg Moran, who did a brilliant job of interpreting my thoughts and translating them into the outstanding graphics in the book.

I am particularly indebted to Mavis Andrews, who edited, designed and managed the project (print version) and provided encouragement as we progressed. The final product is a testament to her outstanding skills and insistence that a quality product be achieved. Mavis you are amazing, and I can't thank you enough.

Finally, I am extremely grateful for my good fortune to be married to my wife, Barb. For over 35 years, she has supported my work with youth, providing helpful critiques of my plans and ideas as well incredible encouragement and understanding, even when my work often took me
away from home. Barb, your encouragement and support throughout the development of this book has been very special to me. You are the love of my life!

— Dave Douglas, December, 2012

ABOUT THE AUTHOR

Dave Douglas has worked with youth, in various leadership roles, for many years—designing, developing, and presenting leadership programs and camps. He works with Rotary sponsored programs such as RYLA (29 years), Interact, Rotaract and Youth Exchange. He has also worked with Scouting Canada as Cub and Scout Master, District Cub Master and Regional Trainer; and with secondary schools in presenting talks and weekend camps on leadership.

Dave is a champion for helping today's youth turn into tomorrow's leaders. He is an accomplished speaker/presenter with over 40 years' experience in senior leadership positions in both the public and private sectors.

Leading the Way is Dave's third published book.

For more information on Dave, visit http://www.leadingtheway-book.com/